My HTC
EVO™ 3D

Lonzell Watson
Craig James Johnston

que®

800 East 96th Street,
Indianapolis, Indiana 46240 USA

My HTC EVO™ 3D

Copyright © 2012 by Pearson Education, Inc.

ISBN-13: 978-0-7897-4909-3
ISBN-10: 0-7897-4909-2

Library of Congress Cataloging-in-Publication Data is on file.

Printed in the United States of America

First Printing: December 2011

Trademarks

Warning and Disclaimer

Bulk Sales

Que Publishing offers excellent discounts on this book when ordered in quantity for bulk purchases or special sales. For more information, please contact

U.S. Corporate and Government Sales

1-800-382-3419

corpsales@pearsontechgroup.com

For sales outside of the U.S., please contact

International Sales

international@pearson.com

EDITOR-IN-CHIEF
Greg Wiegand

ACQUISITIONS EDITOR
Michelle Newcomb

MANAGING EDITOR
Kristy Hart

PROJECT EDITOR
Anne Goebel

DEVELOPMENT EDITOR
Charlotte Kughen,
The Wordsmithery LLC

COPY EDITOR
Christal White,
Language Logistics, LLC

INDEXER
Lisa Stumpf

PROOFREADER
Kathy Ruiz

TECHNICAL EDITOR
Christian Kenyeres

PUBLISHING
COORDINATOR
Cindy Teeters

BOOK DESIGNER
Anne Jones

COMPOSITOR
Bronkella Publishing

Contents at a Glance

Table of Contents

6   Emailing **151**

7   Browsing the Web **183**

About the Authors

Lonzell Watson has been fascinated with technology ever since he disassembled his first Commodore 64 computer in grade school and then attempted to put it back together. He went on to work a 100-mile paper route for an entire year, just to buy his first Apple computer, and he has been writing about technology ever since. After paying his way through college by creating his first mobile computer service and repair company named CompuClean, Lonzell went on to work as an IT consultant for clients including the J. Peterman Company, Time Warner Communications, and Verizon Wireless.

Lonzell is the award-winning author of *Teach Yourself Visually iPad*, for which he won the 2010 International Award of Excellence from the Society for Technical Communication. This work also earned Lonzell the Distinguished Technical Communication award and Best of Show 2010 from the STC. Lonzell was also presented the Award of Excellence for *Teach Yourself Visually iPhoto '09* in 2009. He is the author of other popular titles, including *Teach Yourself Visually iPad 2*, *My Samsung Galaxy Tab*, *Canon VIXIA HD Digital Field Guide*, *Final Cut Pro 6 for Digital Video Editor's Only*, and *Teach Yourself Visually Digital Video*.

Currently, Lonzell teaches Digital Asset Creation to graduate students at Bellevue University and is a freelance technical writer and instructional designer whose courseware has been used to train the CIA, FBI, NASA, and all branches of the U.S. Armed Forces. He is a frequent contributor to StudioMonthly.com and is an author for Lynda.com. Lonzell's writing has been syndicated, with hundreds of published tutorials and tips that help demystify consumer electronics and software. He holds a master's degree in Instructional Design and Development and is the owner of Creative Intelligence LLC, an instructional design and technical writing company (creativeintel.com).

Craig James Johnston has been involved with technology since his high school days at Glenwood High in Durban, South Africa, when his school was given some Apple II Europluses. From that moment technology captivated him, and he has owned, supported, evangelized, and written about it.

Craig has been involved in designing and supporting large-scale enterprise networks with integrated email and directory services since 1989. He has held many different IT-related positions in his career ranging from sales support engineer to mobile architect for a 40,000-smartphone infrastructure at a large bank.

In addition to designing and supporting mobile computing environments, Craig writes about it for BYTE Magazine at BYTE.com and CrackBerry.com, a leading BlackBerry blog. Craig also cohosts the CrackBerry.com, BYTE Wireless Radio, and BYTE Apple Radio podcasts. You can see Craig's previously published work in his books *Professional BlackBerry*, *My BlackBerry Curve*, *My Palm Pre*, *My Nexus One*, *My Motorola Atrix 4G*, and *My BlackBerry PlayBook*.

Craig also enjoys high-horsepower, high-speed vehicles and tries very hard to keep to the speed limits while driving them.

Originally from Durban, South Africa, Craig has lived in the United Kingdom, the San Francisco Bay Area, and New Jersey where he now lives with his wife, Karen, and a couple of cats.

Dedication

To my wonderful wife Robyn for keeping me strong as I write through all hours of the night, and to my late father, Henry Edward Watson, on whose shoulders I stand tall.

—Lonzell Watson

Acknowledgments

I would like to thank the entire *My HTC EVO 3D* team for all of their hard work on this project. I would like to give special thanks to Michelle Newcomb, without whom this project would not have been possible. I would also like to thank my agent Carole Jelen for all of her hard work and insight, as well as my technical editor Christian Kenyeres. Special thanks go to Laura Clor, to Kim Rusher, to my lovely wife Robyn, to Shannon Johnson, and Danya and Sean Platt.

—Lonzell Watson

I would like to thank Stephanie Vinge from Sprint who rushed me an EVO 3D so I could complete some of the chapters.

—Craig Johnston

We Want to Hear from You!

As the reader of this book, *you* are our most important critic and commentator. We value your opinion and want to know what we're doing right, what we could do better, what areas you'd like to see us publish in, and any other words of wisdom you're willing to pass our way.

As an associate publisher for Que Publishing, I welcome your comments. You can email or write me directly to let me know what you did or didn't like about this book—as well as what we can do to make our books better.

Please note that I cannot help you with technical problems related to the topic of this book. We do have a User Services group, however, where I will forward specific technical questions related to the book.

When you write, please be sure to include this book's title and author as well as your name, email address, and phone number. I will carefully review your comments and share them with the author and editors who worked on the book.

Email: feedback@quepublishing.com

Mail: Greg Wiegand
         Editor-in-Chief
         Que Publishing
         800 East 96th Street
         Indianapolis, IN 46240 USA

Reader Services

Visit our website and register this book at quepublishing.com/register for convenient access to any updates, downloads, or errata that might be available for this book.

FriendStream
Widget

In this chapter, you learn about the external features of the EVO 3D and the basics of getting started. Topics include the following:

- → Your EVO 3D's external features
- → Fundamentals of Android
- → Installing synchronization software

Getting to Know Your EVO 3D

Let's start by getting to know more about your EVO 3D. This chapter covers the device's external features and how the Android operating system works.

Your EVO 3D's External Features

The outside of your EVO 3D is what you'll be touching first, so let's go over the external features including the buttons and cameras.

- **Proximity sensor**   Detects when you place your EVO 3D against your ear to talk, which causes it to turn off the screen to prevent any buttons from being pushed inadvertently.

- **Light sensors**   Adjust the brightness of your EVO 3D's screen based on the brightness of the ambient light.

- **Front-facing camera**   A 1.3 megapixel camera for taking self portraits or engaging in a video chat.

- **Earpiece**

- **Power button**   Press once to wake up your EVO 3D. Press and hold for one second to reveal a menu of choices. The choices enable you to put your EVO 3D into silent mode, airplane mode, or power it off completely.

• **Touchscreen**   The EVO 3D has a 4.3" 540×960 pixel Super LCD (Liquid Crystal Display) screen with capacitive touch. The screen is also an auto-stereoscopic display with a parallax barrier that allows it to produce 3D images and video.

How Does the Parrallax Barrier Produce 3D?

Your EVO 3D uses a special technology so that you can see 3D images and video without needing to wear glasses. Read how the Parrallax Barrier technology works here at www.popsci.com/gadgets/article/2011-03/how-it-works-3-d-tv-without-glasses.

• **Volume Up/Down button**   Controls audio while playing music, watching a video, or talking on the phone.

• **Camera Mode button**   This button enables you to switch the camera between 3D and 2D modes. In 2D mode, only the camera toward the edge of the EVO 3D is used as opposed to both.

• **Back button**   Touch to go back one screen when using an application or menu. This soft button doesn't actually press in. When you touch it, your EVO 3D vibrates briefly to let you know it has detected the touch.

• **Menu button**   Displays a menu of choices. The menu differs based on what screen you are looking at and what application you are using.

• **Home button**   Touch to go to the Home screen. The application you are using continues to run in the background.

• **Search button**   Touch to type or speak a search term. Your EVO 3D searches your phone and the Internet for content that matches the search term.

Dual 5 megapixel cameras with autofocus

Dual LED (Light Emitting Diode) camera flash

3.5mm headphone jack

Speakerphone

- **Dual 5 megapixel camera with autofocus** Takes clear pictures close-up or far away. In 3D mode the cameras take 2 megapixel pictures, whereas in 2D mode the one camera takes a 5 megapixel picture.

- **Dual LED (Light Emitting Diode) camera flash** Helps to illuminate the surroundings when taking pictures in low light.

- **Speakerphone** Audio is produced when speakerphone mode is in use. Keep your EVO 3D on a hard surface for the best audio reflection.

- **3.5mm headphone jack** Standard 3.5mm headphone jack allows you to plug in any industry standard headphone or headset.

Micro-USB port

- **Micro-USB port** Use the supplied Micro-USB cable to charge your EVO 3D Incredible or connect it to a computer to synchronize multimedia and other content.

Fundamentals of Android

Your EVO 3D is run by an operating system called Android. Android was created by Google to run on any smartphone, and there are quite a few that run
on it today. Android works pretty much the same on all smartphones with
small differences based on the version of Android installed and the interface
tweaks that each manufacturer has made. Your EVO 3D is running the
Gingerbread version of Android with enhancements added to it by HTC using
the HTC Sense User Interface (UI). Read on to find out how to use Android on
your EVO 3D with the HTC Sense UI enhancements.

The Unlock Screen

If you haven't used your EVO 3D for a
while, the screen goes blank to conserve battery power. To unlock your
EVO 3D, do the following:

1. Press the Power button.

2. Slide the ring toward the middle of
   the screen. This unlocks your EVO 3D.

3. Slide the Phone icon into the ring
   to unlock your EVO 3D and immediately run the Phone app.

4. Slide the Mail icon into the ring to
   unlock your EVO 3D and immediately run the Mail app.

5. Slide the Camera icon into the ring
   to unlock your EVO 3D and immediately run the Camera app.

6. Slide the Messages icon into the ring
   to unlock your EVO 3D and immediately run the Messages app.

Modify Your EVO 3D's Lock Screen

To change how the lock screen looks and which app shortcuts are available, from the Home screen, touch the Personalize icon and then touch Lock Screen. (See the figure in the next task for the location of the Personalize icon.) Choose a lock screen from the available selections and touch Settings to modify which app shortcuts are shown.

The Home Screen

After you unlock your EVO 3D, you are presented with the Home screen. The Home screen contains application icons, a Launcher icon, status bar, and widgets.

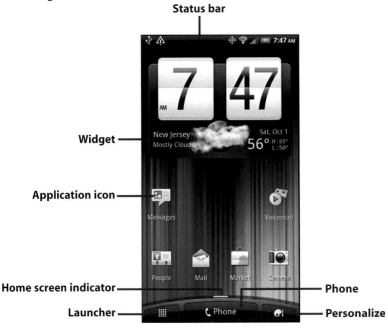

- **Widget**   Application that runs right on the Home screen. A widget is specially designed to provide functionality and real-time information to the Home screen. An example of a widget is one that shows the current weather or provides a search capability.

- **Application icon**   These are application icons that have been dragged to the Home screen from the Launcher. When you touch one, it launches the associated application.

- **Launcher**   Touch to show application icons for all applications you have installed on your EVO 3D.

- **Status bar**   Shows the time, signal strength, battery level, and which type of network you are connected to: Wi-Fi or cellular. Also shows any notification icons, such as New Mail.

- **Phone**   Touch to launch the Phone app.

- **Personalize**   Touch to personalize your EVO 3D. Read more about customizing your EVO 3D in Chapter 12, "Customizing Your EVO 3D."

- **Home screen indicator**   Indicates which of the seven Home screens you are currently viewing. Swipe left and right to move between Home screens.

Drag the Status Bar

You can drag the status bar down to see more notifications or more details on the notifications. When the status bar has been pulled down, touch a notification to be taken to the appropriate application. Touch Clear to clear all notifications. Touch Quick Settings to get to enable and disable your EVO 3D's radios such as Wi-Fi, Mobile Network, 4G, Bluetooth, and GPS, as well as see how much memory is free.

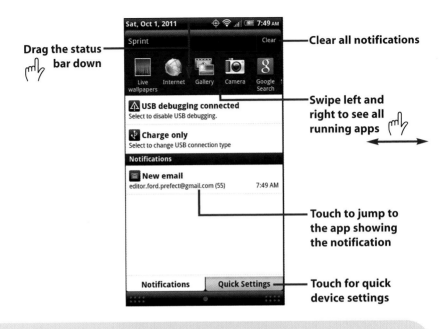

Drag the status bar down

Clear all notifications

Swipe left and right to see all running apps

Touch to jump to the app showing the notification

Touch for quick device settings

>>> Go Further

JUMP BETWEEN HOME SCREENS

You can quickly jump between Home screens by bringing up the thumbnail view of all of the screens. To do this, use the pinch gesture on the Home screen. You see thumbnails of all of the screens. Touch the thumbnail of the screen you want to switch to.

Touch a screen to jump to it

Using Your EVO 3D's Touchscreen

You mostly interact with your EVO 3D by touching the screen—what's known as making gestures on the screen. You can touch, swipe, pinch, double-tap, and type.

- **Touch**   To start an application, touch its icon. Touch a menu item to select it. Touch the letters of the onscreen keyboard to type.

- **Touch and hold**   Touch and hold to interact with an object. For example, if you touch and hold a blank area of a Home screen, a menu pops up. If you touch and hold an icon, you can reposition it with your finger.

- **Drag**   Dragging always starts with a touch and hold. For example, if you touch the status bar, you can drag it down to read all of the status messages.

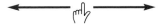

- **Swipe or slide**   Swipe or slide the screen to scroll quickly. To swipe or slide, move your finger across the screen quickly. Be careful not to touch and hold before your swipe or you will reposition something.

- **Double-tap**   Double-tapping is like double-clicking a mouse on a desktop computer. Tap the screen twice in quick succession. You can double-tap a web page to zoom in to part of that page. Double-tap also works in the camera application. Double-tap to zoom the camera.

- **Pinch**   To zoom in and out of images and pages, place your thumb and forefinger on the screen. Pinch them together to zoom out or spread them apart to zoom in (unpinching). Applications such as Browser, Gallery, and Maps currently support pinching.

- **Rotate the screen**   If you rotate your EVO 3D from an upright position to being on its left or right side, the screen switches from portrait view to landscape view. Most applications honor the screen orientation. The Home screen does not.

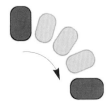

Using Your EVO 3D's Keyboard

Your EVO 3D has a virtual or onscreen keyboard for those times when you need to enter text. You might be a little wary of a keyboard that has no physical keys, but you will be pleasantly surprised to see how well it works. Let's go through the main points of the keyboard.

Some applications automatically show the keyboard when you need to enter text. If the keyboard does not appear, touch the area where you want to type, and the keyboard slides up ready for use.

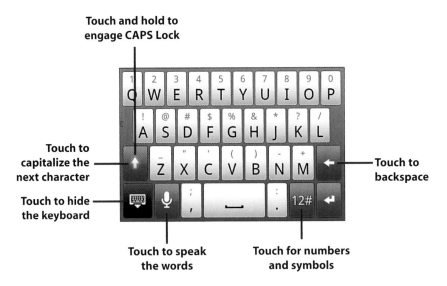

To make the next letter you type a capital letter, touch the Shift key. To make all letters capitals (or CAPS), touch and hold or double-tap the Shift key to engage CAPS Lock. Touch Shift again to disengage CAPS Lock.

To backspace or delete what you have typed, touch the key with the left-pointing arrow. To type numbers or symbols on the virtual keyboard, touch the Symbols key.

Using the virtual keyboard as you type, your EVO 3D makes word suggestions. Think of this as similar to the spell checker you would see in a word processor. Your EVO 3D uses a dictionary of words to guess what you are typing. If the word you were going to type is highlighted, touch space or period to select it. If you can see the word in the list but it is not highlighted, touch the word to select it.

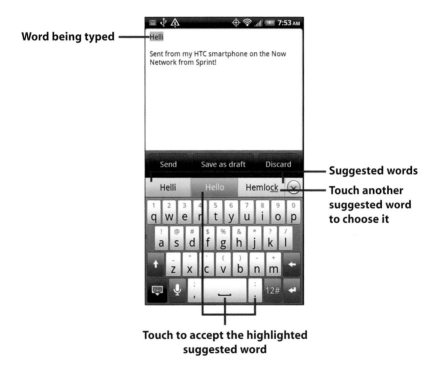

Word being typed — Helli

Suggested words

Touch another suggested word to choose it

Touch to accept the highlighted suggested word

Add Your Word

If you want to save a suggested word to your dictionary, touch the down arrow on the row of suggested words to add the word you are typing to the dictionary.

When on the Number and Symbols screen, touch the 1/2 key to see extra symbols. Touch the ABC key to return to the regular keyboard.

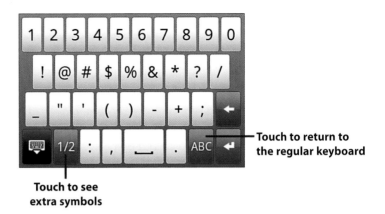

Touch to return to
the regular keyboard

Touch to see
extra symbols

To enter an accented character, touch and hold any vowel or C, N, or S keys. A small window opens enabling you to select an accented or alternative character.

Touch a character
to type it

Touch and hold
for accented
characters

To reveal other alternative characters, touch and hold any other letter, number, or symbol.

Want a Larger Keyboard?

Turn your EVO 3D sideways to switch to a landscape keyboard. The landscape keyboard has larger keys and is easier to type on.

Speak Instead of Typing

Your EVO 3D can turn your voice into text. It uses Google's speech recognition service, which means that you must have a connection to the cellular network or a Wi-Fi network to use it.

1. Touch the Microphone key.

2. The microphone pops up. Wait for the message "Speak now" and start speaking what you want to be typed. You can speak the punctuation by saying "comma," "question mark," "exclamation mark," or "period."

3. After you have spoken what you want to type, you briefly see "working," and then your text is placed in the text field. The text remains underlined so you can touch the backspace key to delete it. If you are satisfied with the text, continue typing on the keyboard or touch the Back button to close the keyboard.

Start speaking when you see this

Touch to cancel

Text you spoke

Swype Keyboard

The Swype keyboard is a revolution-
ary keyboard that enables you to
swipe your finger over the keyboard
to type as opposed to touching each
key individually. Theoretically this
enables you to type more quickly.
The Swype keyboard is preinstalled
on your EVO 3D. Here is how to
switch to the Swype keyboard.

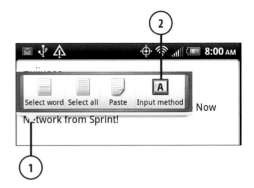

1. Touch and hold in the text entry
   area.

2. Touch Input Method.

3. Touch Swype.

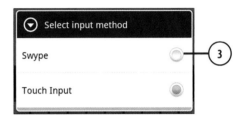

BASICS OF SWYPE

>>> Go Further

There is a full tutorial on how to use Swype on your EVO 3D, but to get you
going, here are the basics:

- Type a word by swiping your finger across all the keys that make up the
  word and then lift your finger.

- To type a double letter (such as the "o" in the word pool), circle the letter
  to be doubled. The Swype keyboard knows to type that letter twice.

- To type an uppercase letter, swipe off the keyboard after swiping over
  the letter and then swipe over the remaining letters in the word.

Editing Text

After you enter text, you can edit it by cutting, copying, or pasting the text. Here is how to select and copy text.

1. Double-tap a word you want to select.

2. Move the green end markers left and right to select more or less text.

3. Touch Copy.

What Can You Do with the Copied Text?

After you have copied some text, you can paste it into any application. To do this, double-tap where you want to paste the text. When the menu pops up, touch Paste.

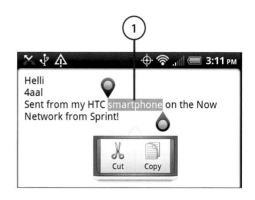

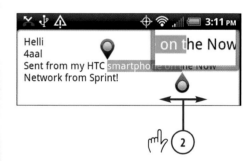

Starting Applications and Application Groups

You can read about applications for your EVO 3D in Chapter 11, "Enhancing Your EVO 3D with Apps," but to get you started, here is how to start applications and switch between them. Each application has an associated icon. Those icons can be on the Home screen or in the Launcher. The Launcher displays every application you have installed.

1. Touch an application icon to launch that application.

2. Touch the Launcher icon to see all installed applications.

3. Swipe up and down to see all apps.

4. Touch to see all applications.

5. Touch to see only favorite applications. The list of favorite applications is automatically created for you based on how many times you open applications.

6. Touch to see only applications you have downloaded.

7. Touch the Menu button to see more options.

8. Touch to see all applications in a list view. Touch again to switch back to the icon view.

9. Touch to remove one or more applications.

10. Touch to change the sort order of the applications when displayed in the Launcher. You can sort them alphabetically, most recent- ly used, or order they were installed.

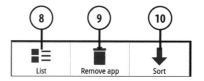

Switch Between Applications

You can quickly switch between recently used applications by touching and holding the Home button. A small window pops up revealing the most recently used applications. Touch an icon to switch to that application.

Menus

Your EVO 3D has two types of menus: Options menus and Context menus. Let's go over what each one does.

Most applications have Options menus. These enable you to make changes or take actions within that application. Sometimes the Options menu has a More item that enables you to see more options. Touch the Menu button to see the Options menu.

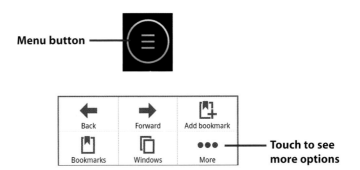

A Context menu applies to an item on the screen. If you touch and hold something on the screen (in this example, a link on a web page), a context-appropriate menu appears. The items on the Context menu are based on the type of object you touch.

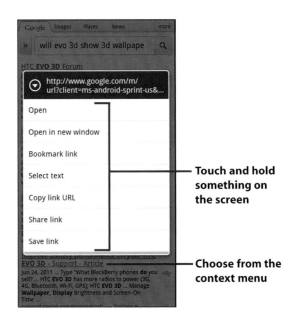

Installing Synchronization Software

Your EVO 3D is designed to work in a disconnected fashion without the need to connect it to your desktop computer. However you might still want to synchronize some content from your computer to your EVO 3D. One of the most common uses for this software is to synchronize music and photos. Examples in this book use an application called doubleTwist. Other applications also provide synchronization for your EVO 3D, such as Missing Sync from Mark/Space, but I've used doubleTwist here because it is free. Before beginning this section, download the version you need (Windows or Mac OSX) from www.doubletwist.com.

Installing doubleTwist on Windows

1. Double-click the doubleTwist install file. On the first screen, click Install.

2. When the install is complete, make sure the Launch doubleTwist box is checked.

3. Click Finish.

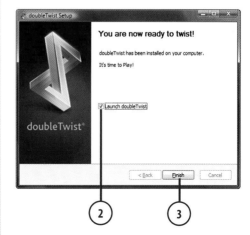

Installing doubleTwist on Mac OSX

1. Double-click the doubleTwist disc on your Mac desktop.

2. Drag the doubleTwist icon to the Applications folder icon.

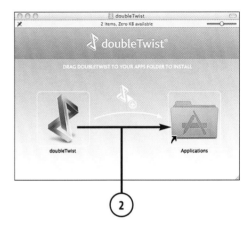

Creating a doubleTwist Account

The first time you run doubleTwist, it asks you to log in using your doubleTwist account. You probably don't have one, so take the following steps to create a free account. The steps and screens are the same for the Windows and Mac versions of doubleTwist.

1. Touch Create Account.

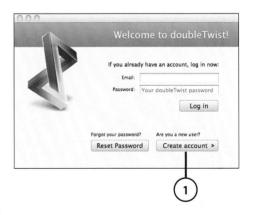

2. Type in your name, choose a password, and type in your email address.

3. Agree to the doubleTwist EULA.

4. Click Sign Up.

5. The next screen tells you to check your mailbox for an activation email. Switch to your email application and follow the instructions in the email. After your account is activated, switch back to this screen and click Continue to start using doubleTwist.

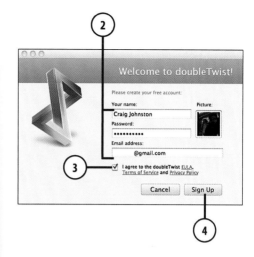

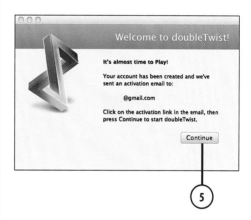

Drag the phone
icon into the ring
to make a call

In this chapter, you learn about your EVO 3D's Phone application. You learn how to place and receive calls, manage them, and use Google Voice as your voicemail. Topics include the following:

2

→ Getting to know the phone application
→ Receiving a call
→ Placing a call
→ Configuring the phone application
→ Google Voice

Using the Phone and Google Voice

As with any good smartphone, your EVO 3D has a great phone that allows for making and receiving calls, managing voicemail, participating in three-way calling, and many other uses. However, your EVO 3D can also use Google Voice to save you money on calls and to transcribe your voicemail if you want it to.

Getting to Know the Phone Application

1. Touch the Phone icon on the Home screen.

2. Enter a phone number or a name using the letters on each number key.

3. Touch to correct a phone number or touch and hold to remove the entire number.

4. Touch to hide the keypad.

5. Touch to display the People application.

6. Touch to dial the number.

7. Indicates the person is already in your contacts.

8. Touch to add the number to an existing contact or create a new contact using the number.

9. Indicates an outgoing call.

10. Indicates an incoming call.

11. Indicates a missed call.

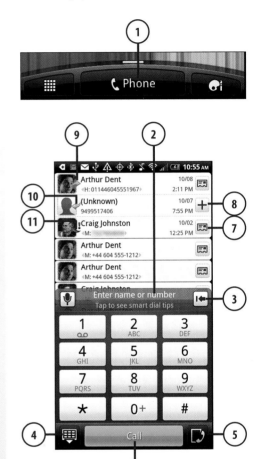

Go Further

PAUSES AND WAITS

To add a two-second pause (symbolized by a "," or a "p"), touch and hold the "*" key until a "p" appears. To add a wait (symbolized by a ";" or a "w") into your phone number, touch and hold the "#" button and wait until a "w" appears. When you add a wait (";" or "w"), your EVO 3D dials the number up to the point of the wait and then waits until it hears a response from the other side. You can insert multiple two-second pauses if you need to. Pauses and waits can be useful when using calling cards, doing phone banking, or dialing into conference calls.

Indicates a pause

Indicates a wait

Touch and hold
for a pause

Touch and hold
for a wait

International Numbers

Normally when you dial international numbers, you have to use some kind of code before the country code. With your EVO 3D, you don't need to know that special code; just type a plus sign, then the country code, then the rest of the number, dropping any zeros before the area code.

Receiving a Call

When you receive a call, you have two choices for handling it.

1. Slide the green icon into the circle to answer the call.

2. Slide the red icon into the circle to send the call to voicemail.

Handling Missed Calls

1. If you miss a call, the missed call icon displays in the status bar.

2. Pull down the status bar to see how many calls you've missed.

3. Touch the missed calls notification to open your EVO 3D's Call Log.

4. Touch the missed call to call the person back.

5. Touch and hold the missed call to see more actions.

6. Touch to view a detailed call history from this number.

7. Touch to call the person back but edit the number dialed first.

8. Touch to see the caller's contact card if the person is already in your Contacts.

9. .Touch to send the caller a text message instead of calling him back.

10. Touch to delete this missed call entry from your call history.

11. Touch to block future calls from this person.

12. Touch to copy the number into your clipboard. You can then paste it into emails and other text entry apps.

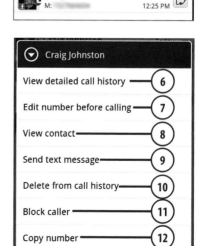

Placing a Call

You can place calls on your EVO 3D in a few ways, including manually dialing a number into the Phone application, touching a phone number in a contact entry, commanding your EVO 3D using your voice, and touching a phone number on a web page, in an email, or in a calendar appointment.

Dialing from a Contact Entry

1. Touch the People application on the Home screen.

2. Touch the name of the person you want to call.

3. Touch the phone number you want to call.

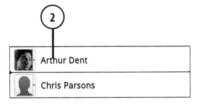

Go Further

DIAL A CONTACT QUICKLY

An alternative method of dialing a contact from the People application is to touch and hold on the contact's name and then choose which number you want to call.

Dialing Using Your Voice

1. Touch and hold the Search button until the Speak Now box appears.

2. Say "Call" and the person's name. For example "Call Arthur Dent." Your EVO 3D finds that person in your Contacts and displays the phone numbers on the screen.

3. Touch the phone number you'd like to call.

Be More Specific

If you know there are multiple phone numbers for a particular contact you want to call, you can be more specific when speaking your command. For example you can say, "Call Arthur Dent at Home," to call Arthur Dent's home number immediately. This reduces the steps needed to place the call.

Bluetooth Support for Voice Dialing

If you are using a Bluetooth headset, hold down the button on your headset for three seconds to activate voice commands on your EVO 3D. Speak a command such as "Call Arthur Dent."

Options While on a Call

While on a phone call, you can mute
and unmute the call, switch the
audio between your EVO 3D and a
Bluetooth headset, bring up the dial
pad, and enable the speaker phone.

1. Touch to end the call.

2. Touch to mute your microphone.
   Touch the button again to
   unmute the microphone.

3. Touch to switch between a
   Bluetooth headset, speakerphone,
   or ear piece.

Need to Know More about Bluetooth?

Read Chapter 5, "Connecting to
Bluetooth, Wi-Fi, and VPNs," for help on
setting up Bluetooth headsets.

4. Touch to view the contact information for the person you called,
   or who called you, as long as it is
   already stored in the People
   application. If the person is not
   listed in your Contacts, you are
   able to add him.

5. Touch to show the dialpad. This is
   useful if you need to use phone
   menus while doing phone banking or dialing into conference calls.

Where Does the Audio Go?

By default, if you are paired with your
Bluetooth headset before you make or
receive a call, the call audio uses the
headset. If you turn your Bluetooth headset on after you are on the call, your EVO
3D automatically switches the audio to it.

Conference Calling

While on a call, you can create an impromptu conference call by adding callers.

1. Touch the Menu button and touch Add Call.

2. A second dialpad appears. Either type in the number for the person to call or touch the Contacts icon to dial from your contacts.

3. Both calls display on the screen. The original call is on hold.

4. Touch to merge the calls together into a three-way conference call.

How to Drop the Second Call

While on a conference call, to drop the last person added to the call, touch the Menu button and touch Flash. This turns the call back into a one-on-one call with the original party.

Can I Drop The Original Call?

If you are on a conference call, you cannot drop the original call you made. In other words, the first person you called cannot be dropped, leaving you on a call with the second person you called. There is no way to do it.

New party is active

Touch to drop the second call

Configuring the Phone Application

You can control how the Phone application works in many ways including whether to display Caller ID information, how to handle call forwarding and call waiting, and changing your voicemail settings.

Call Settings

1. From the Home screen, touch the Menu button and touch Settings.

2. Touch Call.

3. Touch to choose a service to handle your voicemails. This is normally your carrier; however, you can use a different service, including Google Voice.

4. Touch to change the voicemail settings.

5. Touch to clear any voicemail notifications (if there are any).

6. Touch to enable hearing aid support.

7. Touch to enable TTY and choose the TTY mode. Enabling TTY enables you to communicate with people who are deaf or hard of hearing. TTY enables you to type back and forth instead of speaking.

8. Touch to enable DDTM mode. This is necessary on phones like the EVO 3D that use the CDMA cellular technology because you cannot have voice and data connections at the same time. Enabling DDTM makes your EVO 3D send calls straight to voicemail instead of interrupting your data connection.

9. Touch to enable voice privacy, which makes your EVO 3D encrypt your phone calls.

10. Scroll down for more settings.

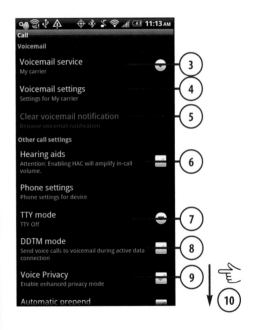

What Is Voice Privacy?

When you enable Voice Privacy, your EVO 3D starts encrypting your calls so that nobody can eavesdrop on them. It's very difficult to eavesdrop on CDMA calls anyway, but it is possible. By encrypting phone calls between your EVO 3D and the cell tower, you add an extra layer of protection on your calls just in case someone wants try to listen in. For this feature to work, your cellular service provider must support it, otherwise enabling it on your EVO 3D is useless.

11. Touch to enable automatic prepend that automatically adds a 1 to long distance calls. This is useful if a number you have chosen to call in the People app is missing the 1.

12. Touch to modify the plus code dialing settings. This enables you to change the international code from its default of 011.

What Is Assisted Dialing?

Assisted dialing, when enabled, helps you dial international numbers while traveling outside your home country. Choose the country you are in as you travel. Assisted dialing is really unnecessary if you always format your phone numbers in the internationally recognized format of +<country code><area code without a leading 1 or 0><number>.

13. Touch to set up one or more Internet calling accounts. Your EVO 3D supports Internet calling using the SIP protocol. The company you work for might offer an SIP service, and you can obtain the information from the IT department to set up your EVO 3D to use it.

14. Touch to select when to use Internet calling.

15. Touch to set the phone settings.

16. Touch to edit default text message that is sent to callers when you don't answer their incoming call.

17. Touch to enable editing the message before sending it.

18. Touch to save unknown contacts to the People app automatically.

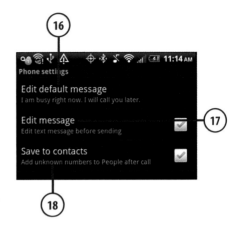

Sound Settings

You can also change the sound settings for calls, such as the ringtone.

1. From the Home screen, touch the Menu button and touch Settings.

2. Touch Sound.

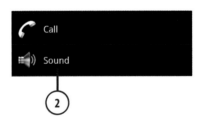

3. Touch to select the default ring-tone to use for incoming calls. This ringtone plays unless you have set a specific custom ringtone for a particular contact.

4. Touch to enable or disable the feature that mutes the ringtone that is playing when it detects you have picked up your EVO 3D.

5. Touch to enable or disable the feature that makes your EVO 3D play the ringtone extra loud when it detects that it is in your pocket.

6. Touch to enable or disable the feature where your EVO 3D enables the speakerphone if it detects you have flipped it over so that the screen is facing down onto a hard surface.

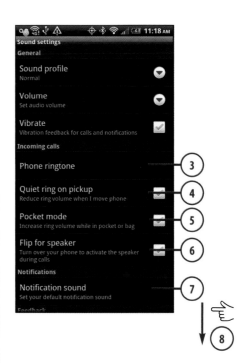

Adding Custom Ringtones

In Step 3 when you touch to select a default ringtone, you can also touch New Ringtone and select an audio file already saved on your phone.

7. Touch to change the default notification sound that plays when a new notification, such as for a missed call, is displayed in the status bar.

8. Scroll down for more settings.

9. Touch to enable or disable audible touch tones when you touch numbers on the phone keypad and whether they play long or short tones.

10. Touch to select whether to enable or disable an alert when you call an emergency number such as 9-1-1. You can select a vibration or a tone to play.

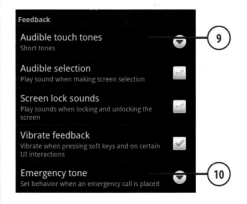

Google Voice

Regular Google Voice, if set up on your EVO 3D, enables you to save money on international calls and have your voicemails transcribed into text. If you upgrade Google Voice, which is free, you have access to some extra features, such as choosing your own personalized phone number or setting up simultaneous ringing.

Setting Up Google Voice

If you want to start using the Google Voice features on your EVO 3D, you need to go through some setup first. If you do not have Google Voice installed, download it from the Android Market. See Chapter 11, "Enhancing Your EVO 3D with Apps," for more on how to use Android Market.

1. Touch the Voice icon on the Home screen.

2. Read the welcome information from Google Voice and touch Next.

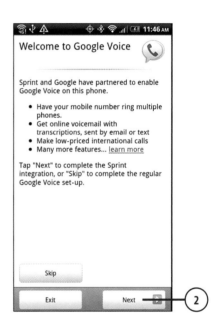

3. Select the account to use for Google Voice if you synchronize to multiple Google Accounts.

4. Touch Sign In to proceed.

5. Touch Allow.

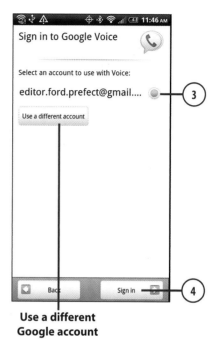

Use a different Google account

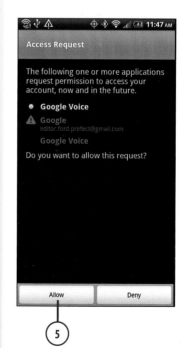

6. Touch Next.

7. Touch Add This Phone.

8. Touch Next to verify your phone number automatically.

9. Touch Next when your number has been verified.

10. Select how you want to use Google Voice.

11. Touch Next.

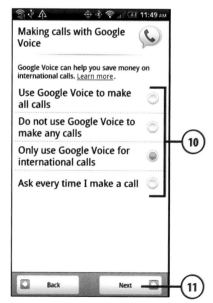

12. Touch Next.

13. Touch the number displayed on the screen if you are told that you must dial a number to configure voicemail. This is carrier-dependent.

14. Touch Configure.

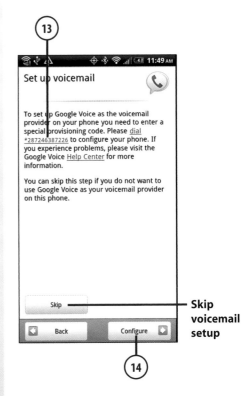

Skip voicemail setup

15. Touch Google Voice.

16. Touch OK.

Upgrading Google Voice

If you want to use the advanced features of Google Voice, you need to upgrade your account. Upgrading is free of charge. To upgrade, use your desktop computer to go to http://google.com/voice and log in using your Google account.

1. Click the cog icon and choose Voice Settings.

2. Click Get a Google Number.

3. Click Continue.

4. Type search criteria in the box to search for available Google Voice phone numbers, including numbers that spell words.

5. Select a number from the options.

6. Click Continue.

7. Click Continue on the Confirm Your Number screen.

8. Enable call forwarding from your current mobile number to your new Google Voice number by following the instructions on the screen and clicking Done.

It Might Cost You

Please be aware that some wireless carriers charge to forward calls, many times on a per-forwarded-call basis, so check with your carrier before enabling the option to forward calls.

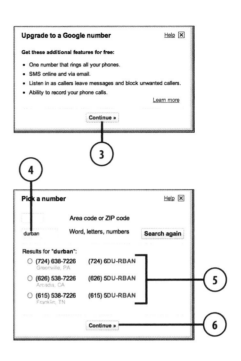

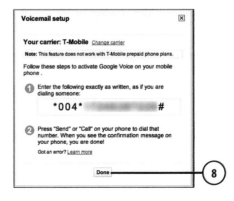

Playing Back and Managing Google Voicemails

When you receive new Google voice-mails, you can find them in your Google Voice Inbox. Launch Google Voice and follow these steps to play them back and manage them.

1. Touch a new voicemail to read it or play back the audio.

2. Touch the play icon to play the message audio.

Sometimes Google Guesses
Grayed-out words in a voicemail transcript are words that Google Voice is unsure of.

3. Touch or press the Menu button to see actions you can take on the voicemail.

4. Touch to call the person who left the voicemail.

5. Touch to send a text message to the person who left the voicemail.

6. Touch to add the person who left the voicemail to People.

7. Touch to mark the person who left the voicemail as one of your favorite contacts.

8. Touch to archive the voicemail.

9. Touch More to refresh the mes-sage or delete it.

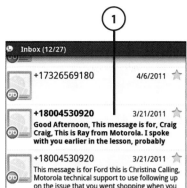

Read the transcript

Activate speakerphone

Send SMS and Check Your Balance

Google Voice enables you to send and receive text (SMS) messages. You can use the main screen menu to do this as well as check your Google Voice account balance and filter the view by label. Touch the Menu button to reveal the menu.

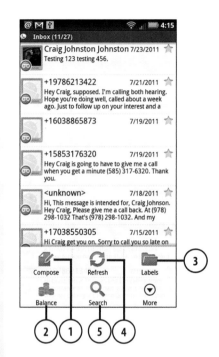

1. Touch Compose to send an SMS. The text message shows your Google Voice number as the sender.

2. Touch Balance to check your Google Voice account balance.

3. Touch Labels to filter the Inbox view by label. Labels include Voicemail, SMS, Recorded, and more.

4. Touch to refresh the Google Voice Inbox.

5. Touch to search the Google Voice Inbox.

Google Voice Settings

After you have been using Google Voice for a while, you might want to change some of the settings.

1. Touch the Menu button and touch More.

2. Touch Settings.

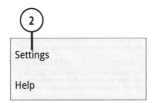

3. Touch to enable or disable Do Not Disturb, which sends all incoming calls to voicemail.

4. Touch to change how you use Google Voice.

5. Touch to select which phones you want Google Voice on.

6. Touch to choose where Google Voice voicemails are played back. Your choices are speakerphone or handset earpiece.

7. Touch to sign out of Google Voice.

8. Touch to configure Google Voice synchronization and notification settings.

Google Voice Sync and Notifications

1. Touch to change how your EVO 3D's background data synchronization is handled. If you disable background synchronization, your Google inbox does not synchronize.

2. Touch to choose where Google Voice text messages are sent. You can choose to only send them to the Google Voice inbox or to also send them to the regular Messaging app.

3. Touch to enable or disable notifications when you receive a new Google Voice text message.

4. Touch to enable or disable notifications when you receive a new Google Voice voice mail message.

5. Touch to enable or disable vibration along with Google Voice inbox notifications.

6. Touch to enable or disable also blinking the notification light when you receive a new item in your Google Voice inbox.

7. Touch to choose a ringtone when a new item arrives in your Google Voice inbox.

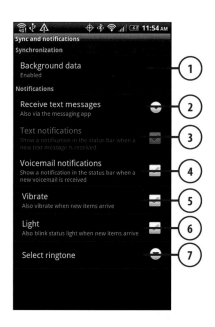

Add, search, manage, and synchronize your contacts

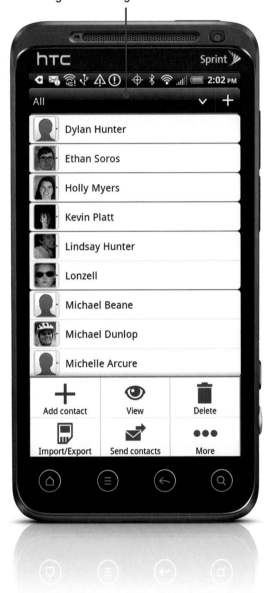

In this chapter, you learn about your EVO 3D's most important application for keeping in touch: People, referred to as "People" on the EVO 3D. You learn how to add, search, manage, and synchronize contacts for quick and convenient access. Topics include the following:

3

→ Exploring the contacts application
→ Adding and managing contacts
→ Exploring contact details
→ Joining and separating contacts
→ Organizing your contacts
→ Sending contact information
→ Communicating with contacts

Managing Contacts

Your EVO 3D is equipped with the People application that can help you manage the personal information for the people you meet, such as phone numbers, addresses, email addresses, websites, and much more. The People application helps you improve your daily efficiency by becoming the central location where you place calls and send texts, multimedia files, and email to personal contacts. You can also synchronize your contacts from other websites such as Facebook and Gmail.

Exploring the Contacts Application

You can manage your communication with contacts with the People app through phone, messaging, and email. You can also view updates of your contacts' Facebook, Flickr, and Twitter accounts. When you synchronize your contacts with your PC, Mac, Google account, or Exchange Server, those contacts are displayed within the People app. If you signed into your Google or Facebook account when you set up your EVO 3D, your contacts from those accounts display when you open the People app.

Adding Accounts

You placed Gmail contacts on your phone when you first activated your EVO 3D using your Gmail account information. You can also add new contacts with the People app, by syncing contacts located on your computer, and by pulling them from your Facebook account.

Transfer Contacts from an Old Phone

You can transfer contacts from your old phone through Bluetooth. Tap the Apps icon on the Home screen and then select Transfer and follow the prompts to move your contacts. You might also be able to transfer calendar events and text messages, depending on the model of your old phone. Bluetooth needs to be enabled for both devices. Refer to Chapter 5, "Connecting to Bluetooth, Wi-Fi, and VPNs," for information on how to connect to Bluetooth on your EVO 3D.

Adding a Facebook Account

If you have a Facebook account, you can synchronize your Facebook contacts' information to your EVO 3D. If any of your Facebook contacts change their information, such as by adding a new contact picture, the picture updates on your phone. Following is how you synchronize your Facebook account.

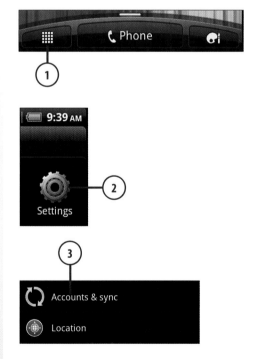

1. Tap the Apps icon on the Home screen.

2. Tap Settings. The Settings screen opens.

3. Tap Accounts & Sync. All accounts you have previously added appear under the Manage Accounts section of the screen.

4. Tap Add Account.

5. Tap Facebook for HTC Sense.

6. Enter the email address you use to log into your Facebook account.

7. Enter your Facebook password.

8. Tap Sign In.

9. Tap your new Facebook for HTC Sense account.

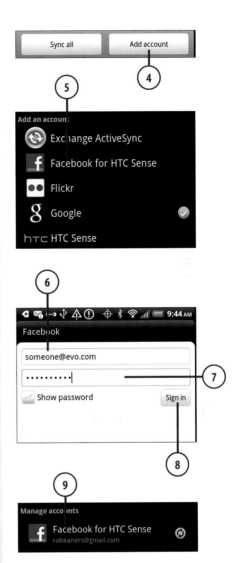

10. Tap to enable or disable live feed synchronization.

Sync Live Feed

The live feed feature for your Facebook homepage enables you to see the latest updates posted by your Facebook friends in real-time. You can enable or disable this feature for Facebook for HTC Sense on your EVO 3D.

11. Tap to add your Facebook calendars to your EVO 3D.

12. Tap to add your Facebook contacts to your EVO 3D.

13. Tap to change the interval for your Facebook for HTC Sense update Schedule.

14. Tap to immediately sync this account.

15. Tap to remove this account from your phone.

Adding a Microsoft Exchange Account

If you have already added a Microsoft Exchange Email to your EVO 3D, depending on how you configured the account on your phone, your Exchange contacts might already be added. If not, you can add an Exchange account so that you can have your work and personal contacts on the same phone, which means you can avoid carrying two.

1. Tap the Apps icon on the Home screen.

2. Tap Settings on the second page. The Settings screen opens.

3. Tap Accounts & Sync. All accounts you have previously added appear under the Manage Accounts section of the screen.

4. Tap Add Account.

5. Tap Exchange ActiveSync.

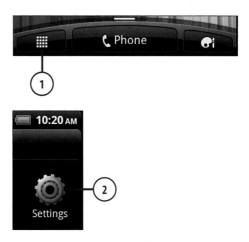

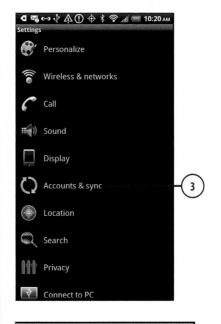

6. Tap Manual Setup.

7. Type your corporate email address.

8. Type in the ActiveSync server address.

9. Type the corporate domain.

10. Type your username.

11. Type your corporate password if it has not been carried over from the previous screen.

12. Tap to enable or disable the use of SSL. This setting is usually enabled.

13. Tap Next.

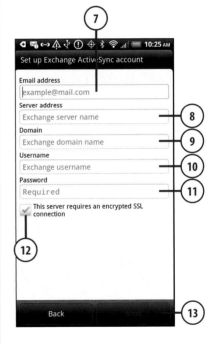

14. Tap to enable or disable the synchronization of mail.

15. Tap to enable or disable the synchronization of your contacts. When you leave this setting enabled, your Outlook contacts sync to your EVO 3D.

16. Tap to enable or disable the synchronization of your calendar.

17. Tap to enable or disable this mail account to automatically check for new email in the corporate inbox and have it delivered to your phone.

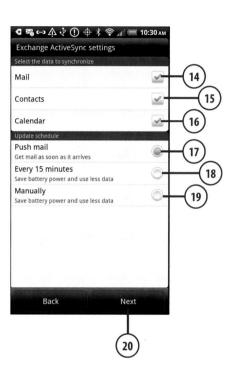

Disabling Push Mail
When you disable the Push mail setting, your EVO 3D only checks for new email messages when you manually access the inbox to a mail account.

18. Tap to change frequency in which email is delivered to your EVO 3D.

19. Tap to enable your phone to check your corporate inbox for new mail and deliver it to your phone only after you access the Mail application.

20. Tap Next.

21. Type a name for this email account.

22. Tap Finish Setup.

Remove an Account
You can remove an account by tapping any account on the Accounts & Sync screen and then choosing Remove Account at the bottom to remove the account.

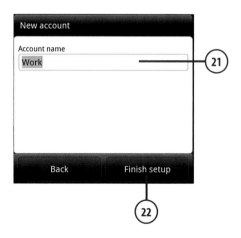

Navigating Your People List

After the People app has been populated with contacts, you have easy access to all of your contacts, and quick access to groups and people you contact the most.

1. Tap the People app. A list of all of your contacts displays on the All screen.

2. Tap the down arrow to filter your contact list and view contacts only from particular accounts such as Google contacts or Facebook contacts.

3. Tap in the search field to search for a contact by entering text or tap the speaker icon to search for a contact by speaking the contact's name.

4. Tap a contact's name, not photo, to open details for a particular contact.

5. Tap a contact's photo to open a menu where you can choose options for communicating with the contact, including Call, Message, and Mail.

6. Indicates when a contact has sent you something, such as a new email, posted live feeds, or when it's the contact's birthday.

Facebook Events

When you link a contact on your phone to his or her Facebook account, the Facebook status or upcoming event appears in that contact.

Google Talk

A green dot appearing to the right of a contact indicates that contact is online in Google Talk. You have to be signed in to Google Talk on your EVO 3D.

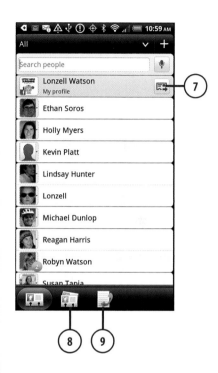

7. Tap to set up, edit, or send your personal profile.

Setting Up Your Profile

When you enter your own personal contact information under My Profile, your information becomes readily accessible and easy for you to share with others.

8. Tap to assign contacts to groups so you can conveniently send SMS, MMS, and email messages to an entire group.

9. Tap to view a call history of all the numbers you have dialed on your EVO 3D.

Display Options

You configure how the People application displays your contacts' information. You can also control which contacts are displayed from which accounts.

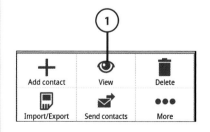

1. Press the Menu button while on the All screen and then select View.

2. Tap to display only contacts with telephone numbers.

3. Tap to choose whether contacts are sorted by first name or last name.

4. Tap to choose whether contact names are displayed first name first or last name first.

5. Tap to search contacts by phone number, email address, company, group name, or all of the above.

6. Tap to enable or disable if contacts are displayed from a particular account.

7. Tap to determine which contacts from a specific account are to be displayed.

8. Tap Done when you are finished.

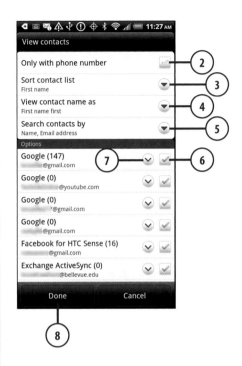

Adding and Managing Contacts

The EVO 3D synchronizes the contact information that you enter into your Google and Exchange accounts automatically. Your EVO 3D automatically tries to combine duplicate contacts if they are named the same or lets you decide which contacts to manually combine. When you send or receive email from individuals who are not in your contacts, you can quickly add them as contacts from within the email client.

Adding Contacts from an Email

The People app streamlines the process for you to add a contact from an email. First, you need to open an email from the sender that you want to add as a contact. Here is how you add a new contact from your Gmail, Email, and Exchange account.

1. Tap the sender's name to open an action menu.

2. Tap to place this contact into one of your groups.

3. Tap Save to Existing Contact if you want to join this contact information with another contact. Consider using this option if the person you are adding uses multiple email accounts under different aliases so that all contact information displays on one detail screen.

4. Select Add Contact to create a new contact entry for this person.

5. Fill out the contacts information. Please refer to the following task "Adding Contacts Manually" to learn more about entering contacts on your device.

6. Tap Save.

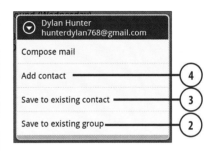

Adding Contacts Manually

You can manually enter contact information for family, friends, and colleagues for quick access and to send messages.

1. From the All screen, tap the Add icon. A new contact sheet opens.

2. Tap to add a picture for the contact from the Gallery or take a picture with the Camera.

3. Type the name of the contact.

4. Tap to add more fields: Name Suffix, Given Name, Middle Name, and Family Name.

5. Tap Contact Type to choose an account to create the new contact under.

6. Tap the + sign in a field to add more contact information. For example, tap the + in the Phone field to add multiple phone numbers.

7. Tap an X to delete a field.

8. Tap the labels within fields to reveal a pop-up menu with other labels to choose from. For example, tap the Mobile label in the Phone field to change it to a Work phone label.

9. Tap the down arrow in the Group field to choose a group in which to place the contact: Co-workers, Family, Favorite, Friends, or VIP.

10. Click to add a date for a birthday, anniversary, or other event.

11. Scroll down to see more fields.

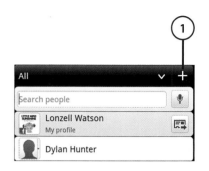

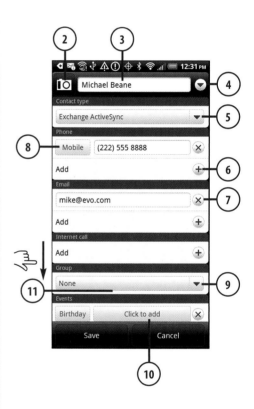

12. Tap a plus sign to reveal more fields to fill.

13. When you are finished adding the contact's information, tap Save.

Edit or Delete an Existing Contact

From the All screen, touch and hold your finger on the contact's name, not picture, and then select Edit or delete from the pop-up menu.

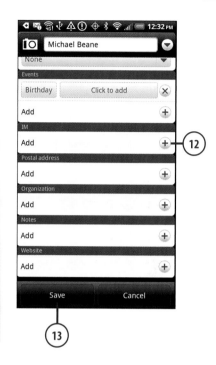

Exploring Contact Details

When you tap a contact on the All screen, the Details screen opens, enabling you to view the information stored for that contact, along with messages and phones calls you have exchanged with that contact. You also have access to Facebook notifications and more from the details screen. Following is how you can navigate the Details screen.

1. Tap the contact's information, not the picture, to access the Details screen.

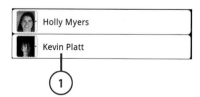

2. Tap the broken link to manually link this contact to another contact in your list.

3. Tap to place a call to the contact.

4. Tap to compose a message in the Messages app to the contact.

5. Tap to choose an email from which to compose a message and send to the contact.

6. Tap to use GPS to locate the contact's postal address.

7. Read the notes that you entered for the contact.

8. Tap to change the ringtone notification for whenever you receive communication from the contact.

9. Tap to block calls from the contact.

10. Tap to edit the information for the contact.

11. Create a people widget on your EVO 3D Home screen for a contact. Tap Set Default Action to control what happens once you tap that widget on your Home screen. The actions are View Contact, Call Mobile, New Message, and Send Mail.

12. Tap to display SMS message exchanges with the contact. You can also reply to a contact's message from this view.

13. Tap to display all email you have received from the contact. You can tap an email to read it.

14. Tap to view the contact's updates and events from accounts you have added from Facebook, Twitter, and Flickr.

15. Tap to view the contact's Facebook and Flickr photo albums.

16. Tap to view your incoming and outgoing call history for this contact. You can tap a listed number to place a call in this view.

17. From the Details view, touch the Menu button to reveal more options and then tap to edit a contact.

18. Tap to delete the contact.

19. Tap to manually link a contact to another contact.

20. Tap to send a contact vCard to another person via SMS, MMS, Mail, or Bluetooth. Think of a vCard as an electronic business card. You can also choose what information is included on the card.

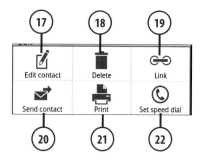

21. Tap to print to a Bluetooth-enabled printer you have added to your EVO 3D.

22. Tap to add the contact's number to speed dial for quick access.

Joining and Separating Contacts

When you synchronize the contacts on your EVO 3D with multiple accounts, such as Gmail, Facebook, Twitter, and Flickr, your EVO 3D tries to join contacts with the same name automatically, or it gives you the option of manually joining contacts. The People app also makes it simple for you to separate joined contacts when necessary.

Joining Contacts Manually

If you have two instances where a contact's name is spelled differently, the People app does not automatically combine them. This can be the case if a person enters only a nickname into his email client or if he simply does not type in his full name, for example. You can join these contacts manually so that so both sets of contact info appear on one Details page. Joining contacts can help you keep your contact information up to date.

1. While on the All screen, tap the contact you want to merge with another contact. The Details page opens.

2. Tap the broken link icon. You could also touch the Menu button and then choose Link in the menu. The Add Contact screen opens.

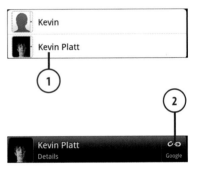

Suggestions on Joining Contacts

If you chose to add a contact that has a similar name to one that is already present in your People list, the People app offers a suggestion on which contacts you might want to join. A broken link with a number appears in the top-right corner of the Details screen. Just tap the link icon to reveal the Suggested Links screen. Tap the broken link to the right of the suggested contact to join the contacts.

3. Tap All Contacts. A list of all contacts on your phone opens.

4. Tap the contact you want to merge.

5. Tap to select a name for the contact. Both contact names appear, and you have to choose one name to represent them both.

6. Tap Done to complete the process.

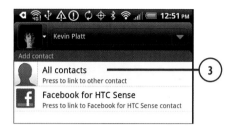

Separating Contacts

In the attempt to automatically join similar contacts, the People app might sometimes get it wrong and link two contacts you do not want together. Perhaps you want two instances of a particular contact to display separately within your list. Here is how you can separate those joined contacts.

1. Tap the contact you want to separate on the All screen.

2. Tap the linked chain icon.

3. Tap one or both of the contacts to separate them. The link icons then appear broken.

4. Tap Done.

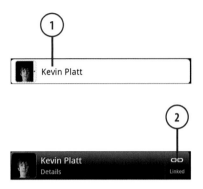

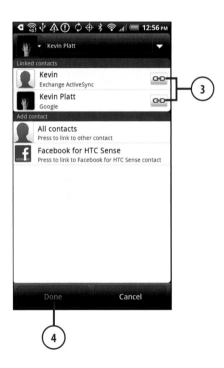

Organizing Your Contacts

When you have all of your contacts on your EVO 3D, you can organize them and share them with others. You can designate your most-used contacts as favorites, create a people widget for a contact on your Home screen, and email vCards.

Adding a Contact to Your Favorites

A faster way to access the contacts that you communicate with most frequently is to add them to your Favorites view.

1. While on the All screen, scroll to the contact you want to add as a favorite and touch and hold your finger to the contact. An action menu appears.

2. Tap Edit Contact.

3. Scroll down to the Groups field and then tap the down arrow.

4. Tap the Favorites group to select it. A green check mark appears.

5. Tap OK to add the contact to your Favorites.

6. Tap Save. Now you can tap the Group view at the bottom of the All screen to access the contact within your Favorites.

People Favorites Widget

Flick your EVO 3D Home screen from left to right for the fastest access to your People Favorites. A People widget listing all your favorites appears, so all you have to do is tap a contact.

Adding a Contact to Your Home Screen

An even faster way to access a contact in the People app is to create a widget for that contact on your Home screen. You can also set the default communication for when you tap the widget.

1. Tap the Personalize icon on the Home screen.

2. Tap Shortcut.

3. Tap Person.

4. Select a contact.

5. Tap View Contact if you want the person's contact detail to display when you tap the shortcut on the Home screen.

6. Tap Call Mobile to place a call to the contact.

7. Tap New Message to have the Messages app open when you tap the shortcut.

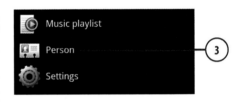

8. Tap Send Mail if you want to access an email account whenever you tap the shortcut on the Home screen.

9. Tap Quick Contact if you want a pop-up menu of all contact possibilities for the contact to display when you tap the shortcut on the Home screen.

Fast Contact Options

The options that appear in the Fast Contact menu are dependent upon the information you have stored for that contact. For example, if you do not have a phone number entered for the contact, the Call option does not appear in the menu.

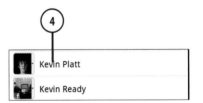

10. The shortcut appears on your Home screen where you can move it to a new location if needed.

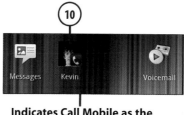

Indicates Call Mobile as the default communication

Sending Contact Information

Instead of typing your contact information when you want to send it to someone, you can send a vCard (a virtual business card) straight from your phone.

1. From the All screen, touch the Menu button and then tap Send Contacts.

2. Tap the contact(s) you want to share to select them. A green check mark appears to the right of each chosen contact.

3. Tap Send.

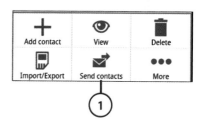

4. Select a send method for the contact. The chosen send option opens so that you can send the vCard.

Send Options May Vary

The options available to Send Contacts vary, depending on how many contacts you select from the list. This is due to varying file sizes. The Bluetooth and Mail options can accommodate more contacts.

Communicating with Contacts

You can call contacts, view their contact information, send them SMS and multimedia messages, mail them, locate their physical addresses on a map, and even write on their Facebook Walls from within the People app. The Fast Contact bar gives you access to these communication options with just one touch of your finger.

1. From the All screen, tap the contact's picture to reveal the Quick Contact bar.

2. Tap Call to place a call to the contact.

3. Tap View to display the contact's details.

4. Tap to open the Messages app to compose a message.

5. Tap Mail to choose an email client in which to compose an email for the contact.

6. Tap Map to pinpoint the contact's physical address on a map and get directions.

Facebook Quick Contact Option

If you have linked a contact to her Facebook account, a Facebook option appears within the Quick Contact bar that enables you to view the contact's Facebook profile.

Communicate via Contact Details

The Details page of each contact also has the same contact options as the Fast Contact bar.

Importing and Exporting Contacts

Along with allowing your contacts to be synced wirelessly, you can also import or export your contacts from your computer as a means of another backup.

Import Contacts from Your Micro-SD Card

You can copy vCard contact information from your computer to your EVO 3D's 2GB micro-SD memory card and then import that vCard information to your phone.

1. From the All screen, touch the Menu button and then select Import/Export.

2. Tap Import from SD Card.

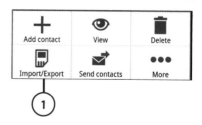

3. Select an account under which the contacts will be created.

4. Select the vCards you want to import.

5. Tap OK to import the contacts.

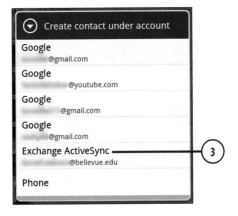

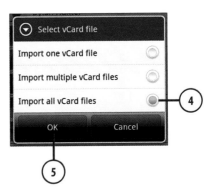

Export Contacts to a Micro-SD Card

You can backup contact information on your EVO 3D to the 2GB Micro-SD memory card of your EVO 3D as another means of backup.

1. From the All screen, touch the Menu button and then select Import/Export.

2. Tap Export to SD Card.

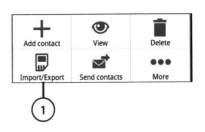

3. Select an account to export.

4. Tap OK to export your contacts list.

Play and manage
audio or video
and record video

In this chapter, you learn how to get the most out of the media and entertainment capabilities of the EVO 3D, including how to manage music and videos, record 3D video, and synchronize media with your computer.

→ Navigating the music application
→ Managing playlists
→ Managing video with the gallery application
→ Recording videos with the camera application
→ Watching TV and movies
→ Watching videos on YouTube
→ Downloading music with Amazon MP3
→ Using doubleTwist to synchronize audio and video

Audio and Video

Your EVO 3D is a digital media player packed with entertainment possibilities as well as a camcorder capable of recording 720p 2D and 3D video. You can play music, movies, TV shows, podcasts, audiobooks, and videos and access YouTube all from your Phone.

Navigating the Music Application

The Music application on your EVO 3D was designed to make it easy for you to browse and play your music collection. A great set of headphones can really enhance your enjoyment of your favorite music. The ability to browse your phone's music library and understanding your playback options are big steps toward getting the most out of your EVO 3D's many entertainment possibilities. Your EVO comes preloaded with eight songs.

1. Tap the Apps icon on the Home screen.

2. Tap the Music app icon located on the second screen of the Apps menu.

3. Tap to access your complete music library. All artists' names are listed.

4. Tap to choose a library in which to browse music: My Library, which is your EVO phone library, or one on a media server.

5. Tap to view the music library as album covers.

6. Tap to view a list of play lists you have created. Please refer to the Managing Playlists section in this chapter to learn how to create a playlist.

7. Tap to view a list of all songs in the library.

8. Slide the panel from right to left to reveal more categories.

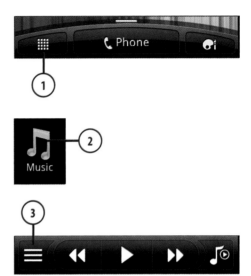

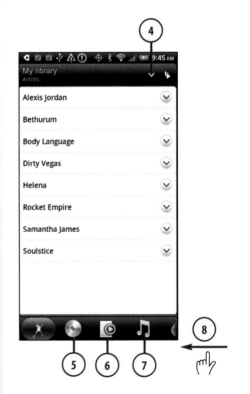

9. Tap to filter the library into Genres.

10. Tap to filter the library into Composers.

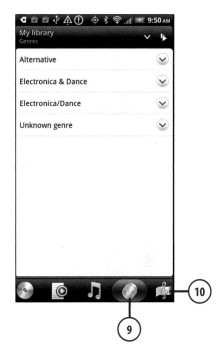

Exploring the Music Application

The Music app provides a number of ways for you to browse your music library, as well as play music from other devices, and control playback. While playing your music, you have some control over how each song is played. Let's take a look at how the Music application works.

1. On the Now Playing screen, tap to play music on another device using Connected Media.

2. Touch and drag the progress bar to jump to any part of the song.

3. Tap to review your complete music library.

4. Tap to go to the previous song in the Now Playing list.

5. Tap to play or pause a song.

6. Tap to go to the next song in the Now Playing list.

7. Tap to switch between the Now Playing screen to the Now Playing list.

8. Tap to turn Shuffle on or off. Shuffle is off when the icon is gray.

9. Tap to cycle through repeat modes. You can repeat all songs or repeat the current song. This is set to Don't Repeat when it is gray.

10. Tap to enhance audio playback performance via SRS sound enhancement. If you are using a wired headset, you have even more options to choose from, such as equalizer settings.

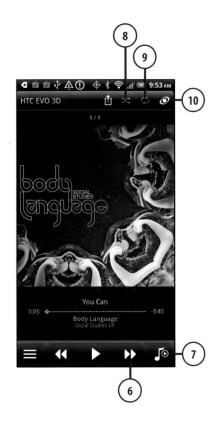

Fewer Options for Bluetooth Headsets

The SRS and equalizer options are not available when you use a Bluetooth stereo headset.

11. Press the volume controller on the right side of your EVO 3D to increase or decrease the volume. A volume window opens, providing a visual representation of the audio level.

Accessing More Actions

While on the Now playing screen, press the Menu button on your EVO 3D to access more Music application options.

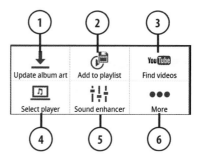

1. Your EVO 3D can locate the cover art for tracks you transferred to your phone from a ripped CD. Tap Update Album Art.

2. Tap to add the current song to a playlist.

3. Tap to find YouTube videos for the current artist you are playing.

4. Tap to play music on another device using Connected Media.

5. Tap to enhance audio playback performance via SRS sound enhancement. If you are using a wired headset, you have even more options to choose from, such as equalizer settings.

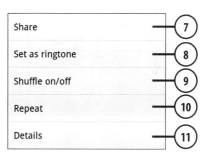

6. Tap to view more options.

7. Tap to share the current track via Bluetooth, Gmail, Mail, and Messages app.

8. Tap to set the track as a phone ringtone or contact-specific ring-tone. A third option is to trim the ringtone, where you drag handles at the start and end points of the song to designate the part you want to use as the ringtone.

9. Tap to turn shuffle on or off.

10. Tap to cycle through repeat modes. You can repeat all songs, repeat one song, or turn Repeat off.

11. Tap to view album details of the current artist.

Working and Listening to Music

You can continue performing other activities on your EVO 3D while your music is playing.

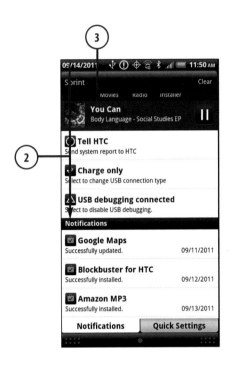

1. Tap the Home button to return to the Home screen and work in another application.

2. Pull down the notification panel to switch back to the currently playing song.

3. Tap the song.

Playing Music from the Lock Screen

When your EVO 3D screen turns off as you are listening to music, you can still control playback from the lock screen. When you wake up your EVO 3D by pressing the Power button, located at the top of the device, the music controls show onscreen. The limited controls on the lock screen enable you to pause, play, and move to the previous and next tracks in the Now Playing list.

Managing Playlists

Playlists are a great way to create a compilation of your favorite songs for playback on your EVO 3D. Use playlists to organize the best songs from your favorite artists, acoustic selections, party music, classic rock, orchestral master-pieces, relaxation tracks, and more.

Creating a New Playlist

The Music app provides a number of ways to browse your music library to select songs to add to playlist.

1. Tap to view the music library.

2. Tap the Playlists category.

3. Tap the Add icon to add a playlist. You can also press the Menu button and choose Add a Playlist from the menu.

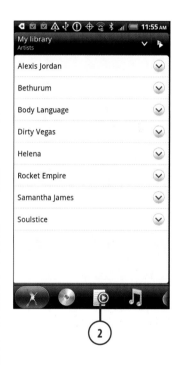

4. Enter a playlist name.

5. Tap Add songs to playlist.

6. Tap the Songs category at the bottom to view a list of all songs.

7. Tap each song that you want to place in the playlist. A green check mark appears to the right of each track to signify it has been selected.

8. Tap Add to add the song(s) to the playlist.

9. An X appears to the right of each added track in the new playlist, allowing you to delete a track if needed.

10. Tap to save the playlist.

Deleting Songs from a Playlist

After you have created a Playlist, you can tap the Playlist category and then press the Menu button on your EVO to remove songs. Tap the Remove Songs option in the menu and then place a check mark next to each track you want to remove. Tap Remove to delete the tracks from playlist.

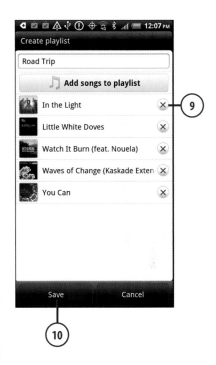

Adding Songs to an Existing Playlist

1. Tap the Playlist category and then tap the name of the playlist to which you want to add songs.

2. Press the Menu button and then tap Add Songs.

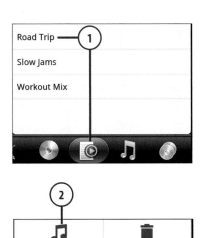

3. Tap the Songs category to browse a complete list of songs or choose your own preferred category to search for songs.

4. Select songs to add to the playlist. Selected songs are identified by a green check mark.

5. Tap Add. The songs are added to the playlist.

Changing the Order of Songs in a Playlist

1. With the playlist open, press the Menu button.

2. Tap Change Order.

3. Use the handle to drag and rearrange the songs within the playlist.

4. Tap Done.

Renaming or Deleting Playlists

1. Tap the Playlist category.

2. Touch and hold your finger on a playlist. A menu appears.

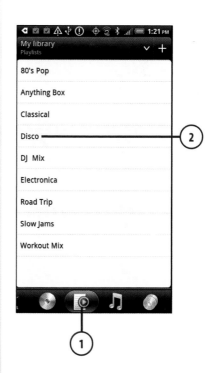

3. Select Rename in the menu to enter a new name for the playlist and save the new name.

4. Tap Delete Playlist to remove one. Deleting the playlist does not delete the songs from your phone.

⊙ Disco

Play

Rename ————————————— ③

Delete playlist

④

Creating a Playlist on a Computer

You can create a playlist within doubleTwist on your computer and then sync that playlist to your EVO 3D. Read the section about doubleTwist later in this chapter to find out how to create a playlist on your computer and sync it to your device.

Managing Video with the Gallery Application

Gallery offers a photo and video management system that also enables you to view, record, delete, and perform basic edits on video. You can also share your videos from Gallery and play your media on a TV screen right from your phone. By default, the Gallery application icon is not located on any of the seven EVO 3D home screens.

② ———— Gallery

1. Tap the Apps icon.

2. Tap to launch the Gallery application.

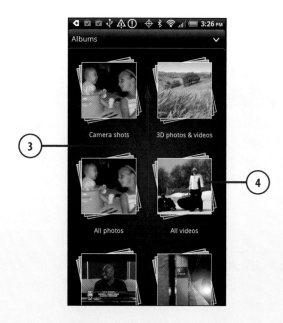

3. Drag your finger up and down to see all albums.

4. Tap All Videos.

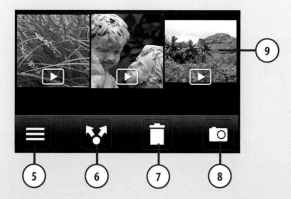

5. Tap to View all albums.

6. Tap to share videos via Bluetooth, Facebook, Flicker, Gmail, Mail Messages, and YouTube.

7. Tap to delete a video.

8. Tap to launch Camera.

9. Tap a video to start playing it.

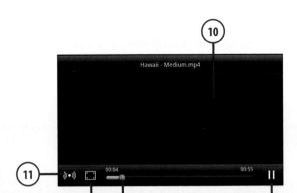

10. Touch the screen to reveal the video controls.

11. Tap to toggle SRS audio effects off and on.

12. Tap to toggle View Full Screen off and on.

13. Touch and drag your finger right or left to jump to any part of the video.

14. Tap to Pause and Play the current video.

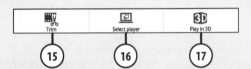

15. Press the Menu button to reveal more options and then tap to perform a basic edit of the video.

16. Tap to select another Bluetooth device as a player.

17. When you are viewing a video that was shot in 3D on your phone, tap Play in 3D to toggle 3D viewing off and on.

Sharing Video Using MMS

Your EVO 3D makes it easy for you to share your video by streamlining the process within Gallery. Here is how you can begin sharing short videos with friends and family in just a few steps.

Message Size Limits

You can only share small videos from your EVO 3D. If your intention is to share a video via MMS, before you begin shooting you need to go into the camera settings and change the video quality to MMS (176×144). The maximum size for a video shot at this resolution is 1019KB. If you attempt to attach a video that is larger, your EVO 3D will more than likely give you a message that the file message size limit has been reached and will not attach the video.

1. Open an album that contains the video you want to share and then tap the Share icon.

2. Select Messages.

3. Select one video to share by tapping it in the album. You are immediately taken to the Messages app.

4. Enter a recipient.

5. Tap to enter a body of text to accompany the video.

6. Tap to send the Message.

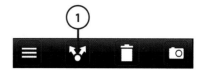

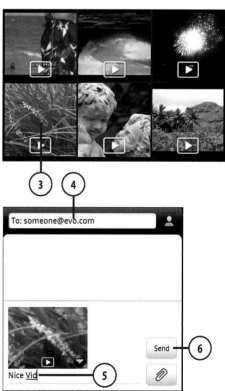

Sharing Video Using Bluetooth

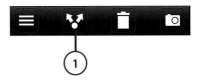

1. Open a video gallery and then tap the Share icon.

2. Select Bluetooth.

3. Select one or more videos to share by tapping them in the album. A green check mark appears in the video(s) you have selected.

4. Tap Next.

Share via

Bluetooth

Facebook for HTC Sense

Flickr

Gmail

Mail

Messages

YouTube

Select one or more items

Next (2)   Cancel

5. Tap Scan for Devices and then choose a previously paired device from the list. If the devices accepts Bluetooth file sharing, the video is sent. Chapter 5, "Connecting to Bluetooth, Wi-Fi, and VPNs," covers how to pair your EVO 3D with Bluetooth devices.

Sharing Video Using Email or Gmail

1. Open an album that contains the video you want to share and then tap the Share icon.

2. Select Gmail or Mail.

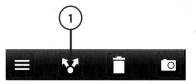

3. Select one or more short videos to share by tapping them in the album. A green check mark appears in the video(s) you have selected.

4. Tap Next to launch the selected email client.

5. Enter the recipient's email address.

6. Tap to enter the subject for the email.

7. Tap to compose a message to accompany the video.

8. Tap to send the email.

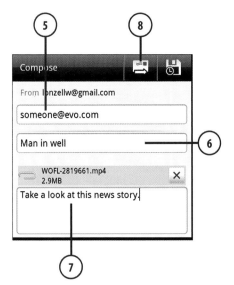

Sharing Video on YouTube

If you do not have a YouTube account, you must first set up a YouTube account before you can upload video to YouTube.com. After you have set up an account, uploading video is a very easy process.

1. Open an album that contains the video you want to share and then tap the Share icon.

2. Select YouTube.

3. Select a video to share by tapping it in the album. A green check mark appears in the video you have selected.

4. Tap Next.

5. If you are asked to do so, enter Your YouTube Username and Password and then sign into your YouTube Account.

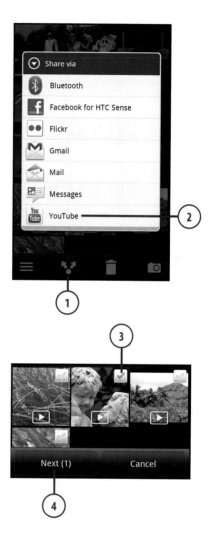

6. Tap to enter a title for the video you are uploading.

7. Tap More Details to enter more information about the video, such as a description and tags, and to select a privacy option.

8. Tap Upload to upload the video to your YouTube account.

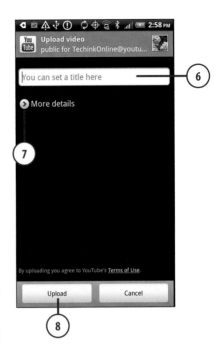

Deleting Videos

1. Open an album that contains the video you want to delete.

2. Tap the delete icon that looks like a trash can.

3. Select the videos you want to delete by tapping them. A red X appears in the video thumbnails that you choose.

4. Tap Delete to remove the video from the albums.

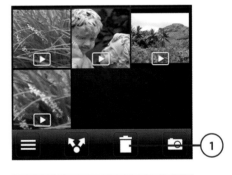

Editing Videos

Your EVO 3D gives you the ability to perform a basic trim for the start and end points of your videos. This function can help you trim down a video file that might be too large to email, or to trim away excess, unwanted video so that the recipient can only view the good stuff.

1. Open an album that contains the video you want to trim and then touch and hold your finger on the video you want to trim.

2. Tap Trim. The Trim window opens.

3. Drag the start and end points toward the center to frame the content that you want to keep in the video.

4. Tap Done to save the video. A trimmed copy of the video is saved within the album, and the original video remains untouched.

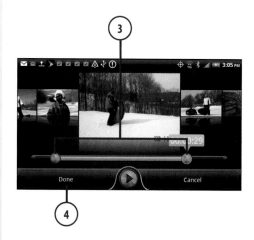

Recording Videos with the Camera Application

Your EVO 3D uses dual 5-megapixel, auto-focusing, rear-facing cameras located on the back of the device, to capture 720p video in 3D or 2D. The EVO 3D is also equipped with a 1.3-megapixel front-facing camera, so you can video chat. Both Photo and Video modes come with a unique group of settings to help you capture the best image.

Recording Video

1. Tap Camera to launch the application. You can also hold the physical camera button on the side of your EVO 3D until you feel a vibration.

2. Tap to switch from the still camera to the video position.

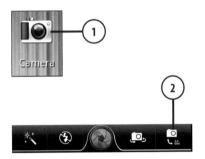

How Do I Take a Picture?

Check out Chapter 10, "Capturing, Storing, and Viewing Photos," to find out how to use the Camera app to take still photos.

---

3. Slide the physical switch on the side of the EVO 3D to select either 2D or 3D recording. For the best 3D video, you must hold your phone in landscape orientation while recording.

4. Drag the Zoom slider to enlarge the framed scene. Be wary of this setting because it degrades the image.

5. Tap in the viewfinder to selectively focus on an area in the shot and to automatically adjust the exposure. You hear a chime after you adjust the focus and exposure.

6. Touch the onscreen Record button or press the physical Camera button on the side of your EVO 3D to begin recording video. Tap the onscreen Record button or press the physical Camera button again to stop recording.

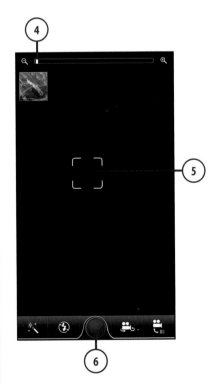

It's Not All Good

Digital Zoom Quality

Your phone has the ability to zoom, but be wary. The EVO 3D uses a 5x digital zoom that simply enlarges a portion of the image to simulate an optical zoom, which degrades the image. Moving physically closer to your subject, when possible, helps get you the highest quality image possible.

Talking About Focus and Exposure

Your EVO 3D automatically focuses on what is in the middle of the viewfinder when you begin recording. Before and while you are recording, tap on the main subject in the viewfinder to adjust the focus for that spot. The EVO 3D also automatically adjusts the exposure for the area you tap on screen.

Changing Video Settings

There are more settings you can adjust that enable you to configure the Camera app before you begin recording video. Your phone is also equipped with some very helpful features commonly found on dedicated video cameras, including a video light to brighten dark scenes, manual and automatic white balance, as well as manual exposure, contrast, saturation, and sharpness controls.

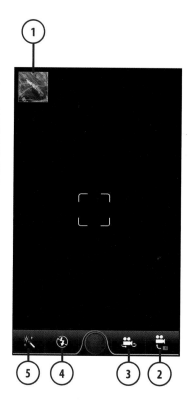

1. Tap to review recorded videos.

2. Tap to switch between video and still camera modes.

3. Tap to switch between back and front-facing cameras.

4. Tap to turn on the video light to brighten dark scenes.

5. Tap to add in-camera effects including Grayscale, Sepia, Negative, and Solarize.

6. Press the Menu button on your EVO 3D to access Settings.

7. Tap to access slide controls that enable you to adjust the Exposure, Contrast, Saturation, and Sharpness of scenes.

8. Tap to change the white balance so that the camera can capture colors more accurately in different lighting environments. The Auto setting works well in most lighting situations.

9. Tap to select a default video resolution to use. Take note that by default, your EVO 3D is not set at the highest resolution possible for your phone, which is 1280×720.

10. After you record a video, your EVO 3D automatically lets you review the video you have just captured and then returns you to the viewfinder screen. Tap this setting to set the time for a recorded video to be displayed on the review screen before the screen changes back to the viewfinder.

11. Tap to turn stereo audio recording Off and On.

12. Scroll down to view more settings.

13. Tap to toggle between recording with or without audio.

14. Tap to reset all settings to their original factory default states.

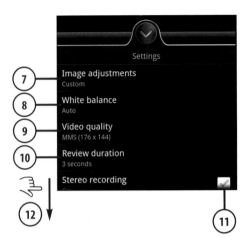

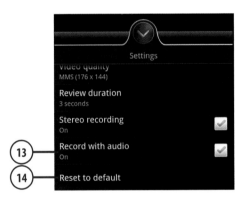

Go Further

ADDING IN-CAMERA EFFECTS

Keep in mind when you use any of the photo or video effects, they become a permanent part of your pictures. To give yourself more choices in the future as to how you will use your images, consider adding effects after you take the photo using the effects options in the Gallery app or by purchasing an Android photo-editing program that enables you to perform such effects after you take the image. This way, you can retain the unprocessed image for more flexible use in the future.

Watching TV and Movies

Your EVO 3D is packed full of entertainment outlets for you to watch free and paid TV programs and also to rent and purchase movies. The Sprint TV & Movies app is a great one-stop-shop for you to access exciting video content. The Blockbuster On Demand app gives you access to a huge library of featured movies.

Sprint TV & Movies

The Sprint TV & Movies app puts LiveTV and On Demand content at your fingertips including movies, premium channels such as ESPN On Demand, Disney XD, ABC Family, Comedy Central, MTV, and Discovery channel. These are just a few of the offerings.

1. Tap the Apps icon on the Home screen.

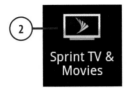

2. Scroll until you find the Sprint TV & Movies application icon and then tap it.

3. If this is your first time starting this app, a message appears informing you that the content is subject to location-based restrictions and requires access to your location information. Tap Accept.

4. You must turn off Wi-Fi before you can view Sprint TV. If you have launched the Sprint TV & Movies app before disabling Wi-Fi, you see a message. Tap Disable Wi-Fi. The Sprint TV & Movies app Home screen opens.

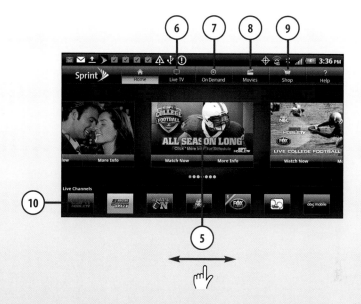

5. Slide your finger right to left to browse through featured shows.

6. Tap to view Live TV listings that are available.

7. Tap to browse on demand television content. Content that you have to pay for is marked with a dollar sign next to each channel listing.

8. Tap to purchase movies.

9. Tap to shop for channel subscriptions.

10. Tap an icon on the Live Channels Section at the bottom of the screen to start viewing Live TV.

Blockbuster On Demand Application

Your EVO 3D enables you to browse and download one of the largest catalogs of movies, including 3D titles with the preloaded Blockbuster On Demand application. There are no monthly fees for this app, just pay as you go. Rentals range from $1.99 to $3.99 and purchases from $5.99 and up. You can set up a Blockbuster On Demand account on your EVO 3D in very little time.

1. Registering involves a bit of typing, so consider creating an account on your computer. Open a browser and go to Blockbuster.com.

2. Click On Demand.

3. Click On Demand Devices.

4. Under MOBILE, click Sprint.

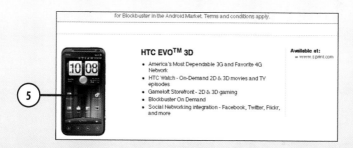

5. Click to activate HTC EVO 3D.

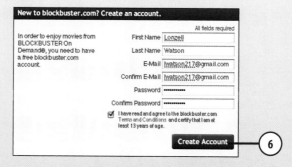

6. Enter your information, click in the box to accept the Terms and Conditions, and then click Create Account.

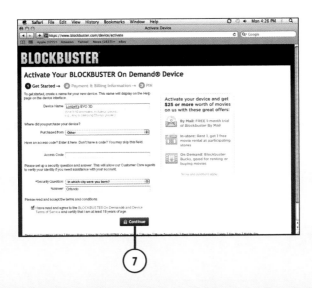

7. Fill out the form and then tap Continue.

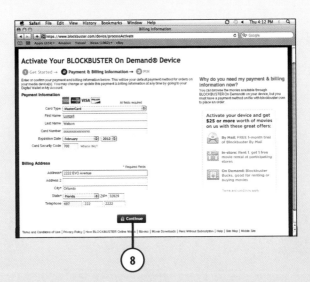

8. Enter your credit card information and billing address then click Continue. You do not need the PIN number to activate your EVO 3D.

9. On your EVO 3D, tap the Apps icon to view the Apps menu.

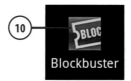

10. Tap the Blockbuster app icon.

11. Tap click to go to Android Market.

12. Tap Update.

13. Tap OK to begin the download. The application updates and then closes.

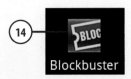

14. Tap the Blockbuster app icon again to open the application. The Blockbuster Main screen opens.

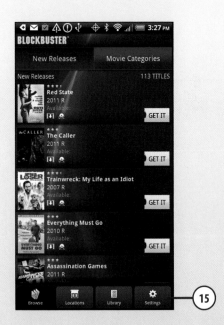

15. Tap Settings.

16. Tap Activate Device.

17. Tap Activate Now.

18. Enter your Email Address and Password for the account and then tap Sign In. Activation is now complete.

19. Tap Go Browse to search for titles.

Finding Movies on Blockbuster and Changing Settings

After you launch the Blockbuster application, there are several ways for you to search content from the home page. You can access the many movie categories of Blockbuster from the home page, as well as browse the collection of movies you have downloaded and tweak settings.

1. Tap Movie Categories to browse the Blockbuster library by movie genre.

2. Tap locations to use your EVO 3D's GPS capability to locate your local Blockbuster.

3. Tap Library to browse the collection of Blockbuster movies you have downloaded.

4. Tap Settings to deactivate your device, instruct the Blockbuster app to use your current GPS location, and to check for new versions of the Blockbuster app. You can also press the Menu button on your EVO 3D from any screen to access the settings screen.

Renting and Purchasing Movies on Blockbuster

The process for renting and purchasing movies is the same. When you have set up a Blockbuster On Demand account and have registered a credit card, you can begin downloading your movie selections in just a few clicks.

1. Browse to the movie you want to rent or purchase and then tap Get It.

2. Tap In Store to check availably of the movie for rent at your local Blockbuster.

3. Tap By Mail to rent the movie and have it mailed to you.

4. Tap On Demand to rent or buy the movie and have it downloaded directly to your phone.

5. Tap to rent or buy the movie.

6. Tap Confirm to rent or purchase the movie and begin download-ing. If you rent the movie, you have 30 days to watch it, and then the movie is no longer accessible from your phone.

The Green Hornet 3D

Your EVO 3D is already preloaded with action feature *The Green Hornet 3D*. Just tap the Apps icon on the Home screen, and the movie is located on the third screen of the menu.

YouTube

The high-resolution screen of the EVO 3D, along with its video cameras, makes it great for viewing and sharing videos online, anywhere and anytime. The preinstalled YouTube widget gives you the ability to browse and view videos posted by users from around the world, as well as upload videos taken with your EVO 3D, as soon as you take them.

YouTube Main Screen

1. Tap Apps icon on the Home screen.

2. Scroll to the last page of the Apps menu and then select YouTube.

3. If the Mobile Terms of Service appear, tap Accept.

4. Tap to play a video.

5. Tap to perform a search for a video.

6. Tap to launch the camcorder and then upload your video to YouTube. The upload process is streamlined when you access the camcorder from here. You must create a YouTube account before you can upload a video.

Playing a Video

While you play a YouTube video, you can rate the video, read comments left by other YouTube members, save a video to your phone, store it in your favorites, share it with others, and more. A variety of YouTube controls are shown, depending on in which orientation you hold your EVO. In the Landscape orientation, you have more screen real estate in which to view videos. Many more controls are shown when you hold your phone in portrait orientation than in the landscape orientation.

1. Tap a video to play it.

2. Tap within the video to pause play-back.

3. Tap the Thumbs-up icon to say you like the video. You can see on the Info tab how many people like and dislike the current video.

4. Tap the Thumbs-down icon to say you dislike the video.

5. Tap More to review more options.

6. Tap Flag to send a message to YouTube concerning a video that displays content that is not in adherence to YouTube's Terms of Service agreement. You must be logged into your YouTube account to flag a video.

7. Tap to save the current video to your phone. You must be logged into your YouTube account.

8. Tap to save the video to your favorites. You must be logged into your YouTube account.

9. Tap to share the video with someone else via Bluetooth Friend Stream, Gmail, Mail, Messages, and Peep.

Other Sharing Options
Other sharing options might appear in this list if you have downloaded apps that allow for additional sharing features.

10. Tap to copy the URL for the video so that you can embed it into another site or to paste it somewhere else.

11. Tap to review a list of videos with similar content to the one you are currently viewing.

12. Tap to read comments left by other YouTube members.

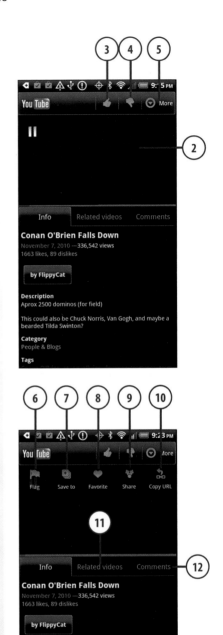

Filtering Videos

When you first launch YouTube, you are presented with a Featured list of videos. You can further filter the vast library of YouTube videos and browse by category.

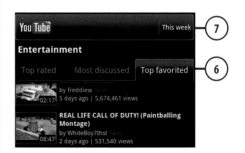

1. Press the Menu button and then tap Browse. The Browse option is available when you press the Menu button from the Home screen and while you are playing a video.

2. Scroll and tap the category you want to browse.

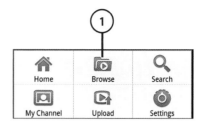

3. Tap to review a list of the top rated videos on YouTube for this week.

4. Tap to review a list of the videos that received the most comments on YouTube for this week.

5. Slide the tabs section from right to left.

6. Tap to review a list of the top favorited videos for this week.

7. Tap to filter categories to display videos older than This Week, including This Month and All Time. When you change this setting, all YouTube screens are affected.

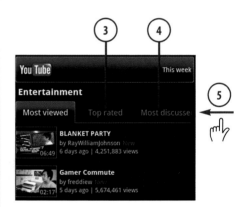

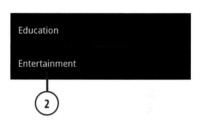

Changing YouTube Settings

If you want to further customize your YouTube experience on your EVO 3D, you can change the default video playback quality, caption font size, clear your search history, and use SafeSearch filtering from within the General Settings.

1. Press the Menu button and then tap Settings.

2. Tap to turn on and off the Start High Quality Video setting for times you are connected to a mobile network.

3. Tap to select a larger or smaller caption font sizes for YouTube videos.

4. Tap to clear your YouTube search history.

5. The YouTube app can be set to block videos containing restricted content from appearing within search results. By default, filtering is set to Moderate. Tap to turn off SafeSearch or set a Strict filter setting.

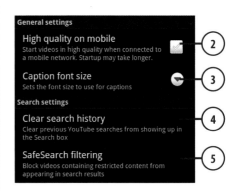

Amazon MP3

Your EVO 3D comes with the Amazon MP3 application that enables you to shop, purchase, and download music from Amazon.com. Cloud Player is also a part of Amazon MP3. Within Cloud Player you can access music stored on your Cloud Drive, enabling you to manage, play, or download music using Amazon's secure online storage space. The Amazon MP3 app icon is located in the Apps menu on the first page. Before you can begin purchasing music, you need to set up an Amazon.com account. If you do not have an Amazon.com account, visit Amazon.com on your computer and create an account.

Setting Up the Amazon MP3 Application

After you have created an Amazon.com account, you are ready to browse, purchase, and download music. Here is how you can set up the Amazon MP3 application with Cloud Player.

1. Tap the Apps icon.

2. Tap the Amazon MP3 icon on the first page.

3. Press the Menu button; tap to return to the Amazon MP3 Home screen, from whichever screen you may be on within the application.

4. Tap to view all of your Amazon MP3 downloads.

5. Tap to go to the Now Playing screen, which features the last track you previously played.

6. Tap to search Amazon MP3 for a track or album.

7. Tap to be taken to the Amazon MP3 website to receive more information on using Amazon Cloud Player.

8. Tap Settings for more options.

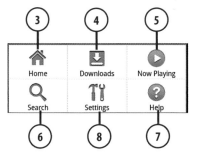

9. Tap to sign out and into your Amazon.com account on your device.

10. Tap to store Amazon gift card and promotional code information.

11. Tap to instruct Amazon MP3 to download content only when your phone is connected to a Wi-Fi net-work to conserve data plan usage.

12. Tap to clear cached songs, album art, and Now Playing queue.

13. Tap to enable or disable Amazon MP3 Lock-screen playback con-trols when your phone is locked.

14. Tap to choose an equalizer setting such as Classical, Dance, Jazz, Pop, and Rock to enhance the type of music that you are currently lis-tening to.

15. Tap Delivery Preference to choose whether future downloads are saved to your phone or your Cloud Drive. (You have to sign into your Cloud Drive for the Amazon Cloud Drive Settings to be accessible.)

16. Tap to automatically download to your phone purchases saved to your Cloud Drive.

17. Scroll down to view more options.

Two Ways to Upload to Your Cloud Drive

When you shop for music in the Amazon MP3 store, you are prompted to save to your Cloud Drive or your phone at the end of each purchase. If you choose to save to your Cloud Drive, you are asked to sign into the Amazon online space. (Find out how to make purchases in the Amazon MP3 store in the following section.) You can also go to www.amazon.com/cloudplayer on your PC or Mac and upload your music collection so that you can enjoy your purchases on all your devices.

18. Tap to designate a particular streaming network preference for playing music files located on your Cloud Drive on your phone.

19. Your Cloud Drive updates every 10 minutes. Tap to manually update your Cloud Drive.

Finding Music

1. Tap Store on the Amazon MP3 Home screen.

2. Touch and enter a search term to search Amazon.com for music.

3. Tap to see the bestselling albums.

4. Tap to see new releases.

5. Tap to browse music by genre.

6. Tap to access Cloud Drive music as well as on-device music.

Now Playing track controls

Purchasing Music

After you have located a song or album that you would like to purchase, you can preview that music before purchasing it and then proceed to buy the music.

1. Tap an album or song to listen to a 30 second preview.

2. Tap the price of the song. The price button turns into a Buy button.

3. Tap Buy.

4. If you are not logged into your Amazon account, you are prompted to do so. Enter your Amazon login information.

5. Tap to agree to the Amazon MP3 Store Terms of Use.

6. Tap Sign In.

7. Tap to save your purchase to your Amazon Cloud Drive to begin setting up your Cloud Drive. If you had chosen to Save to this device, the download would take place.

8. Read the Cloud Player Terms of Use and then tap to accept the terms.

9. Tap Continue to begin setting up your Amazon Cloud Drive and save your purchase.

Using doubleTwist to Synchronize Audio and Video

You can transfer music collections that you have on your computer with your EVO 3D by connecting your phone as an external drive or by using software such as doubleTwist. If you have not installed doubleTwist, please follow the directions in the prologue.

Running doubleTwist and Mounting Your EVO 3D

You need to use the supplied USB cable to connect your EVO 3D to your Mac or PC. When you connect your EVO 3D to your computer, you can choose a connection type that allows your phone to charge only or connect as a disk drive.

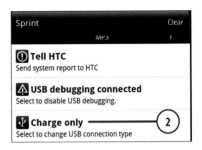

1. Connect your EVO 3D to your computer using the USB cable. The connection type screen is accessible, but you have to unlock your phone to see it.

2. Slide to unlock your phone and then choose to connect as a Disk drive. If you waited too long to make a choice on the connection screen, the screen disappears, but you can pull down the Notification panel and then tap the default Charge Only setting to reset the connection type.

3. Tap the Disk Drive option.

4. Tap Done at the bottom to connect to your computer.

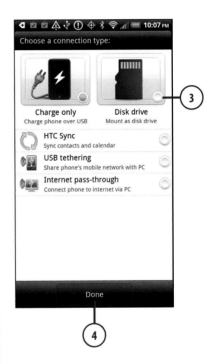

Synchronizing Music by Dragging Files

After you have connected your EVO to your computer and your phone is visible in doubleTwist, you can copy music by simply dragging and dropping files.

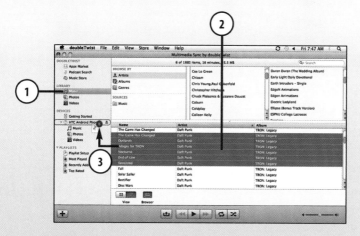

1. In doubleTwist, click Music to view all of the music on your computer.

2. Find and select the song(s) you want and copy to your EVO 3D.

3. Drag the file(s) to your EVO 3D located under Devices. A red icon should appear when your mouse is over the EVO icon, indicating the number files transferred. When you drop the files, the music is copied to your phone.

It's Not All Good

Usage Restrictions

Some of the music in your Library is Digital Rights Management (DRM) protected, which means their use has been restricted. The files are noted with a lock icon within Multimedia Sync. These music files are from a time when music was not DRM free on iTunes. You won't be able to transfer these songs without upgrading them for a fee. Visit the iTunes Store for more information.

Synchronizing Existing Playlists

If you use iTunes to manage your music collection on your computer, you might have already created playlists that you would like to import into doubleTwist.

doubleTwist makes it easy for you to import iTunes Playlist.

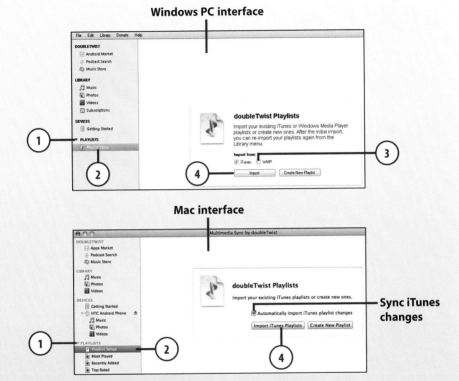

Windows PC interface

Mac interface

Sync iTunes changes

1. Click Playlists to reveal the playlists.

2. Click Playlist Setup.

3. If you are on a PC and you don't use Windows Media Player to manage your music, deselect WMP on your PC.

4. Click Import if you are using a PC. (Click Import iTunes Playlists if you are using a Mac.) Your iTunes Playlists appear in the sidebar.

Sync iTunes Changes

If you are using a Mac, you can select Automatically Import iTunes Playlist Changes to keep your Multimedia Sync playlists in sync with changes you make in iTunes.

Windows PC interface

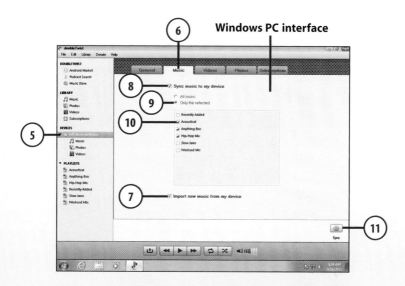

Mac interface

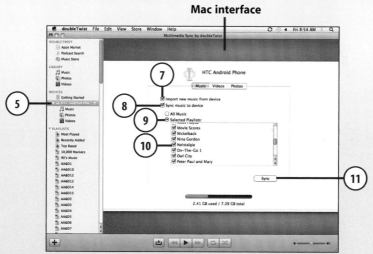

5. Click your EVO 3D in the Devices list.

6. If you are using a PC, select the Music tab. If you are using a Mac, skip to step 7.

7. Select Import new music from device to import music from your EVO 3D to your computer.

8. Select Sync Music to My Device.

9. Select the Only the Selected option, if you are using a PC. Select the Selected Playlists option for a Mac.

10. Select the playlist(s) you want to sync.

11. Click Sync. The new music on your EVO 3D is now synced to your computer, and the playlists you selected are synced to your EVO 3D.

Drag and Drop

You could have also dragged and dropped the playlists you wanted from the sidebar area to your EVO 3D in the Devices list.

Creating Playlist

If you do not use iTunes and therefore will not be synchronizing iTunes playlists with doubleTwist, you can create new playlists from within doubleTwist by taking the following steps.

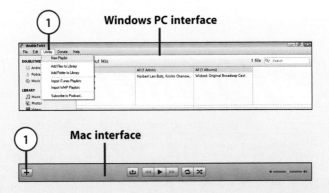

1. Click in the Playlist section, go to Library if you are using a PC, and then select New Playlist. On a Mac, click the New Playlist button.

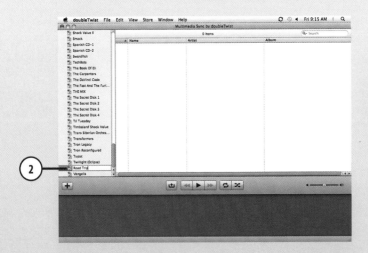

2. Enter the name of the new playlist.

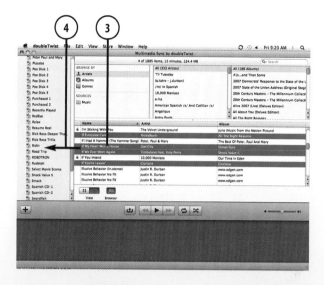

3. Locate the music you would like to use for the playlist on your computer in the Music Section of doubleTwist.

4. Drag the music to your new playlist. When you are finished adding songs, repeat the steps in the Synchronizing Existing Playlist section to sync the new playlist to your EVO 3D.

Access Amazon MP3 Within doubleTwist

doubleTwist has a portal to the Amazon MP3 website that enables you to browse, purchase, and download your favorite music to your computer and then sync them to your phone. Just click the Music Store option located in the sidebar under doubleTwist.

Copying Video

doubleTwist has a great feature that saves you the step of having to manually convert video files on your computer so that they work on your mobile phone. doubleTwist automatically optimizes videos by converting the screen size and CODEC when you drag and drop video files from your computer to your EVO 3D.

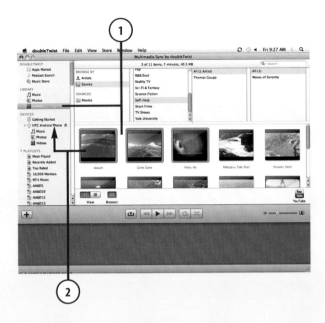

1. Click Videos under Library in doubleTwist and locate the video(s) that you want to copy to your EVO 3D.

2. Drag the video(s) to your EVO 3D. If the video is located in your iTunes archive, regardless if it has no DRM, you will not be able to copy it to your phone.

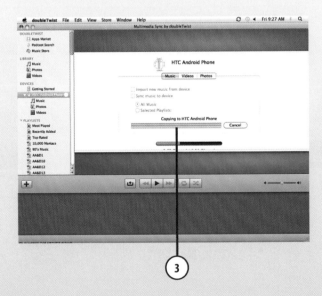

3. A progress bar is displayed within doubleTwist to represent the progress of the video transcoding process.

Sprint Radio

In addition to Amazon MP3, your EVO 3D also offers a variety of listening pleas-
ures via the Sprint Radio app. You have access to 100+ radio stations including
talk, news, and music from a variety of genres, such as pop, urban, rock, hip-hop,
and Latin. You can find the Sprint Radio app icon in the Apps menu.

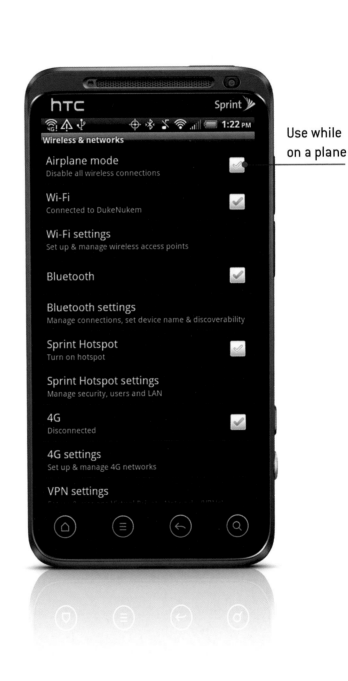

Use while
on a plane

In this chapter, you learn about your EVO 3D's connectivity capabilities including Bluetooth, Wi-Fi, VPN, and web browsing. Topics include the following:

5

→ Connecting to Bluetooth devices
→ Connecting to Wi-Fi networks
→ Using Virtual Private Networks (VPNs)
→ Turning your EVO 3D into a Wi-Fi hotspot

Connecting to Bluetooth, Wi-Fi, and VPNs

Your EVO 3D can connect to Bluetooth devices such as headsets, computers, and car in-dash systems, as well as to Wi-Fi networks, and 2G, 3G, and 4G (WiMax) cellular networks. It has all the connectivity you should expect on a great smartphone. Your EVO 3D can also connect to virtual private networks (VPN) for access to secure networks. Your EVO 3D can even share its 3G or 4G cellular connection with other devices over Wi-Fi.

Connecting to Bluetooth Devices

Bluetooth is a great personal area network (PAN) technology that allows for short distance wireless access to all sorts of devices such as headsets, other phones, computers, and even car in-dash systems for hands-free calling. The following tasks walk you through pairing your EVO 3D to your device and configuring options.

Pairing with a New Bluetooth Device

Before you can take advantage of Bluetooth, you need to connect your EVO 3D with that device, which is called *pairing*. After you pair your EVO 3D with a Bluetooth device, they can connect to each other automatically in the future.

1. Tap the Menu button and then tap Settings.

2. Tap Wireless & Networks.

3. Tap to enable Bluetooth.

4. Tap Bluetooth Settings.

5. Tap Device Name to change the name your EVO 3D uses when it identifies itself to the Bluetooth network. Your EVO 3D's real model number is PG86100, and this is used to identify your EVO 3D when you pair with other Bluetooth devices. You could change it to something more personal, such as Craig's HTC EVO 3D.

6. Tap Discoverable if you want to make your EVO 3D discoverable on the Bluetooth network. Your EVO 3D remains discoverable for 120 seconds (two minutes). Making your EVO 3D discoverable is necessary when someone else is trying to pair with your EVO 3D.

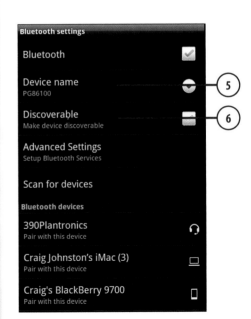

7. Tap Scan for Devices to get your EVO 3D to scan the Bluetooth network for other Bluetooth devices. If your EVO 3D finds any other devices, they are listed on the screen. In this example, a Bluetooth headset, a BlackBerry, and a computer have been found.

8. To pair with a Bluetooth device, tap the device. In this example, we are pairing with the Plantronics headset.

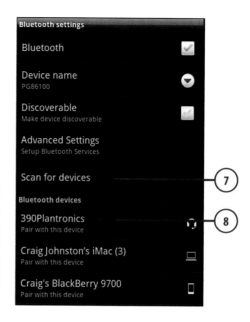

Bluetooth Passkey

If you are pairing with a device that requires a passkey, such as a car in-dash system or a computer, the screen shows a passkey. Make sure the passkey is the same on your EVO 3D and on the device you are pairing with. Tap Pair on your EVO 3D to confirm the passkey on the device you are pairing with.

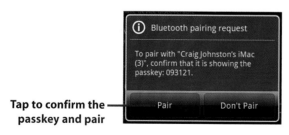

Tap to confirm the passkey and pair

9. If all went well, your EVO 3D should now be paired with the new Bluetooth device.

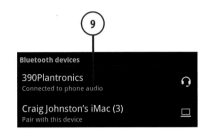

All Zeros

If you are pairing with an older Bluetooth headset, you might be prompted to enter the passkey. Try using four zeros or four ones as the passkey. It normally works. If the zeros or ones don't work, refer to the headset's manual.

Changing Bluetooth Options

After a Bluetooth device is paired, you can change a few options for some of them. The number of options depends on the Bluetooth device you are connecting to. Some have more features than others.

1. Tap and hold on a Bluetooth device to see available options.

2. Tap to disconnect from the Bluetooth device.

3. Tap to disconnect and unpair from the Bluetooth device. If you do this, you won't be able to use the device until you redo the pairing as described in the previous task.

4. Tap for more options.

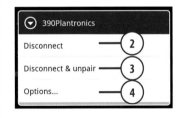

5. Tap to connect with the Bluetooth device if you are currently disconnected from it.

6. Tap to enable and disable using this device for phone calls. Sometimes Bluetooth devices have more than one profile. You can use this screen to select which ones you want to use.

Bluetooth Profiles

Each Bluetooth device can have one or more Bluetooth profiles. Each Bluetooth profile describes certain features of the device. This tells your EVO 3D what it can do when connected to it. A Bluetooth headset normally only has one profile, such as Phone Audio. This tells your EVO 3D that it can only use the device for phone call audio. Some devices might have this profile but provide other features such as a Phone Book Access profile, which would enable it to synchronize your EVO 3D's address book. The latter is typical for car in-dash Bluetooth.

Quick Disconnect

To quickly disconnect from a Bluetooth device, tap the device on the Bluetooth Settings screen and then tap OK.

Advanced Bluetooth Settings

Your EVO 3D has two extra Bluetooth features that might prove useful to you. It can become a Bluetooth FTP server, and it supports the Message Access Bluetooth profile. Here is how to enable and configure these two features.

1. Tap Advanced Settings.

2. Tap to enable or disable the Bluetooth FTP Server.

3. Tap enable or disable the Message Access Profile.

4. Tap to change the Message Access settings.

5. Tap to enable or disable support for sending email messages to another device via Bluetooth.

6. Tap to enable or disable support for sending SMS (text messages) to another device via Bluetooth.

What Is Bluetooth FTP Server?

Bluetooth FTP Server, when enabled, allows people using devices that also support the Bluetooth FTP Profile browse the external MicroSD memory card in your EVO 3D. They can delete files, browse the files, and upload files. The first time someone tries to access your EVO 3D via the FTP Profile, you are prompted to accept it. If you want a quick way to access files sent to your EVO 3D using this feature, from the Home screen tap the Personalize icon (bottom right), tap Folder under Add Items to Home, and tap Bluetooth Received.

Tap to always accept this device

Tap to accept this device

What Is Message Access?

Bluetooth Message Access is a Bluetooth Profile that enables you to exchange email and SMS (text messages) with other Bluetooth devices that support the Message Access Profile. This is normally supported by car in-dash systems so that they can automatically receive emails and SMSs and read them to you while you drive.

Wi-Fi

Wi-Fi (Wireless Fidelity) networks are wireless networks that run within free radio bands around the world. Your local coffee shop probably has free Wi-Fi, and so do many other places such as airports, train stations, and malls. Your EVO 3D can connect to any Wi-Fi network and provide you higher Internet access speeds than the cellular network.

Connecting to Wi-Fi

The following steps explain how to find and connect to Wi-Fi networks. After you have connected your EVO 3D to a Wi-Fi network, you automatically are connected to it the next time you are in range of that network.

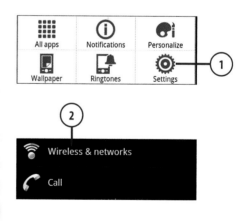

1. Tap the Menu button and tap Settings.

2. Tap Wireless & Networks.

3. Tap to enable Wi-Fi.

4. Tap to change Wi-Fi Settings and connect to Wi-Fi networks.

5. Tap to turn on or off your EVO 3D's Wi-Fi radio.

6. Tap Network Notification to enable or disable the notification that tells you a new open Wi-Fi network is available.

7. Tap a Wi-Fi network to connect to it.

Tap to connect using WPS

Tap to add a hidden network

Adding a Hidden Network

If the network you want to connect to is not listed on the screen, it might be purposely hidden. If it is hidden, it does not broadcast its name, which is also known as its SSID. You need to tap Add a Network, type in the SSID, and choose the type of security that the network uses. You will need to get this information from the network administrator ahead of time.

Type in the SSID to connect to a hidden network

What Is Wi-Fi Protected Setup (WPS)?

WPS is a standard that enables you to securely connect to a Wi-Fi network with little or no participation from you. WPS is designed to handle the entire process of connecting to the network on its own. Many times the Wi-Fi network router you are connecting to has a WPS button on it. You simply press the button and then tap Wi-Fi Protected Setup on your EVO 3D and you will be connected.

8. If the Wi-Fi network is secure, you receive a prompt to enter a password or encryption key.

9. Tap Connect to continue.

10. If all goes well you see the Wi-Fi network in the list with the word Connected under it.

Can't Connect to Wi-Fi?

If all does not go well, you might be typing the password or encryption key incorrectly. Verify this with the person who owns the Wi-Fi network. Sometimes there is a lot of radio interference that causes problems. Ask the person who owns the Wi-Fi network to change the channel it operates on and try again.

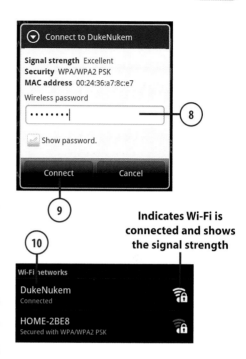

Indicates Wi-Fi is connected and shows the signal strength

Wi-Fi Network Options

1. Tap a Wi-Fi network to reveal a pop-up that shows information about your connection to that network.

2. Tap Forget to tell your EVO 3D to not connect to this network in the future.

3. Tap and hold on a Wi-Fi network to reveal two actions.

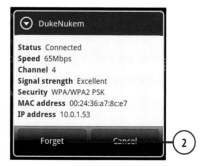

4. Tap to forget the Wi-Fi network and no longer connect to it.

5. Tap to change the Wi-Fi network password or encryption key that your EVO 3D uses to connect to the network.

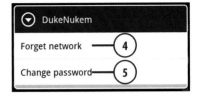

Advanced Wi-Fi Options

Your EVO 3D enables you to configure a few advanced Wi-Fi settings
that can actually help preserve your
battery life.

1. Tap the Menu button while on the Wi-Fi Settings screen and tap Advanced.

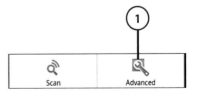

2. Tap to change the Wi-Fi sleep policy. This enables you to choose if your EVO 3D automatically turns off Wi-Fi. Because Wi-Fi is more efficient than 3G and is free, you should leave this set to Never.

3. Tap to enable or disable a Wi-Fi feature that boosts the Wi-Fi range of your EVO 3D. This is useful if you are far away from the Wi-Fi router. It does drain the battery faster, though, so be careful.

4. Tap to setup and configure a Wi-Fi Proxy. A Wi-Fi Proxy is a server on the network that handles data that is not destined for the default gateway.

5. Use this Wi-Fi MAC address if you need to provide a network administrator with your MAC address in order to be able to use a Wi-Fi network.

6. Tap Use Static IP to force your EVO 3D to use a static IP address and static network access settings.

7. Set the IP address, Gateway, and Subnet mask for your EVO 3D if you are choosing to use a static IP in Step 6.

8. Scroll down for more options.

9. Tap to enable or disable a feature that lets your EVO 3D choose its own IP address if one is not automatically assigned to it.

Wi-Fi Is More Efficient and Free

Believe it or not, Wi-Fi is more efficient than a 3G or 4G cellular network. The more time you can keep the Wi-Fi radio on and can be connected to a Wi-Fi network, the longer your battery lasts. If you have a valid data connection via Wi-Fi, your EVO 3D actually stops using the cellular 3G or 4G network. So while at home, why not set the Wi-Fi sleep policy to Never. Unless you have an unlimited data plan, it is also a good idea to use Wi-Fi whenever possible because it is free.

WHY USE A STATIC IP OR MAC?

>> Go Further

First, what are an IP address and a MAC address? A MAC address is a number burned into your EVO 3D that identifies its Wi-Fi adapter. This is called the physical layer because it is a physical adapter. An IP address is a secondary way to identify your EVO 3D. Unlike a Physical Layer address or MAC address, the IP address can be changed any time. Modern networks use the IP address when they need to deliver some data to you. Typically when you connect to a network, a device on the network assigns you a new IP address. On home networks, this is typically your Wi-Fi router.

In rare circumstances, the Wi-Fi network you connect to might not assign your EVO 3D an IP address. In these circumstances, you need to ask the network administrator to give you a static IP address.

Some network administrators use a security feature to limit who can connect to their Wi-Fi network. They set up their network to only allow connections from Wi-Fi devices with specific MAC addresses. If you are trying to connect to such a network, you have to give the network administrator your MAC address, and he adds it to the allowed list.

Cellular Network Settings

Your EVO 3D can connect to 2G (CDMA 1X), 3G (EVDO Rev A), and 4G (WiMax) cellular networks.

Changing Mobile Settings

Your EVO 3D has a few options when it comes to how it connects to cellular (or mobile) networks.

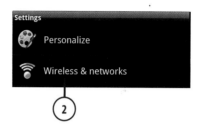

1. Tap the Menu button and tap Settings.

2. Tap Wireless & Networks.

3. Tap to enable or disable connecting to the Sprint 4G WiMax network.

4. Tap to see information about the 4G network you are connected to, including the network provider (if you are roaming), signal strength, and your IP address.

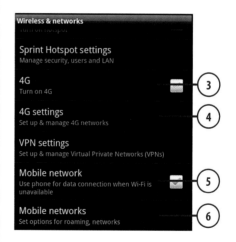

5. Tap to enable or disable the mobile network.

6. Tap Mobile Networks to change options.

7. Tap to enable or disable a feature that plays a sound when you connect to a mobile network that is not your home network.

8. Tap to enable or disable warning messages to be displayed when you are roaming and use voice or data services.

9. Tap to change the roaming mode. You can change it to only roam on the Sprint network, or to allow your EVO 3D to connect to any compatible CDMA network.

10. Tap to enable or disable the ability to make and receive voice calls while roaming.

11. Tap to enable or disable the ability to use cellular data services while roaming.

12. Tap to enable or disable the ability to make and receive voice calls while roaming.

13. Tap to enable or disable the ability to use cellular data services while roaming.

14. Tap to enable or disable always-on mobile data.

Should I Disable Always-On Mobile Data?

If you disable always-on mobile data, you can save on battery life. However, you effectively kill the functionality of any app that needs to be connected all the time, such as Instant Messaging apps (Yahoo!, Google Talk, and so on) or apps such as Skype. You also stop receiving email in real time. When this feature is disabled, about five minutes after your EVO 3D goes to sleep, it disconnects from the mobile data network, but it remains connected to the mobile voice network.

Virtual Private Networks (VPN)

Your EVO 3D can connect to virtual private networks (VPNs), which are normally used by companies to provide a secure connection to their inside networks or intranets.

Adding a VPN

Before you add a VPN, you must first have all the information needed to set it up on your EVO 3D. Speak to your network administrator and get this information ahead of time to save frustration. This information includes the type of VPN protocol used, type of encryption used, and the name of the host to which you are connecting.

1. Tap the Menu button and tap Settings.

2. Tap Wireless & Networks.

3. Tap VPN Settings.

4. Tap to add a new PPTP, L2TP, or IPSec VPN.

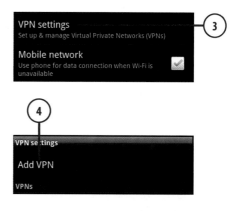

5. Tap the VPN technology your company uses.

6. Go through each section and enter the information your network administrator gave you.

7. Tap the Menu button and tap Save to save the VPN settings.

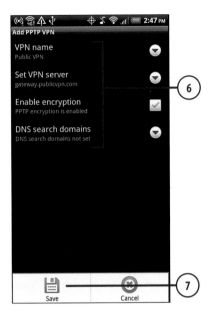

Connecting to a VPN

After you have created one or more VPN connections, you can connect to them when the need arises.

1. Follow steps 1–3 in the "Adding a VPN" section to navigate to the VPN Settings screen.

2. Tap the VPN you want to connect to.

3. Enter your username and password.

4. Tap to allow your EVO 3D to remember your VPN username.

5. Tap Connect. After you're connected to the VPN, you can use your EVO 3D's web browser and other applications normally, but you now have access to resources at the other end of the VPN tunnel, such as company web servers or even your company email.

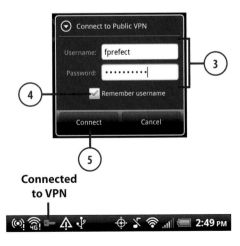

Connected to VPN

>> Go Further

EDIT OR DELETE A VPN

You can edit an existing VPN or delete it by tapping and holding on the name of the VPN. A window pops up with a list of options. From here you can edit the VPN's settings or delete the VPN.

Tap and hold the VPN

Edit or delete the VPN

Sprint Hotspot

Your EVO 3D has an application called Sprint Hotspot that enables you to use Wi-Fi to share your EVO 3D's 3G or 4G Internet connection with up to eight other devices. This feature only works with an optional extra monthly fee, which covers the extra data you use when this feature is enabled.

Starting Your Sprint Hotspot

1. Tap to launch Sprint Hotspot.

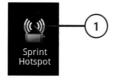

2. Enter a unique name for the Wi-Fi network you create when you enable this feature or leave it as the default.

3. Tap to select the type of security you want to use on the Wi-Fi network or select No Security. It is a good idea to use security so that the people who connect to your hotspot have encrypted data going over the air.

4. Enter the password or key you want to use on your hotspot to encrypt the data.

5. Tap to start your hotspot.

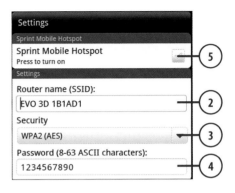

After Your Hotspot Is Started

After you start your Hotspot, provide the Router name (SSID), Security, and Password to anyone who you want to allow to connect. In the notification bar you will see the 3G Mobile Hotspot icon indicating that your Hotspot is working. Tap Manage Users to see who is connected.

Tap to see who is connected

Advanced Settings

Sometimes you want to have some more control over your 3G Mobile Hotspot, such as changing the Wi-Fi channel, or you might want to control who can connect.

1. Tap Manage Users before you start your hotspot.

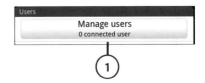

2. Tap to enable or disable a feature that lets you decide who can connect to your hotspot. When this is enabled, you are prompted to allow or block connection requests.

3. Tap to choose how many people can connect to your hotspot. You can have up to eight connections.

4. Tap Done to save your settings.

5. Tap the Menu button and then Advanced to see the advanced hotspot settings.

6. Tap to change the number of minutes after which your hotspot automatically disables itself if it detects no activity.

7. Tap to change your hotspot's LAN settings. Only change the LAN settings if you have an understanding of IP.

8. Tap to choose the IP address of your Wi-Fi hotspot.

9. Tap to change the subnet mask of the IP address.

10. Tap to enable or disable the ability for your Wi-Fi hotspot to automatically assign IP addresses to devices that connect.

11. Tap to choose the starting IP address that your Wi-Fi hotspot uses when it automatically assigns addresses.

12. Tap to reset the LAN settings.

HotSpot Sucks Power

When you use Sprint Hotspot, it is a good idea to keep your EVO 3D plugged in to the wall or to a car charger. This is because Sprint Hotspot uses a lot of power and CPU cycles and drains your battery very quickly.

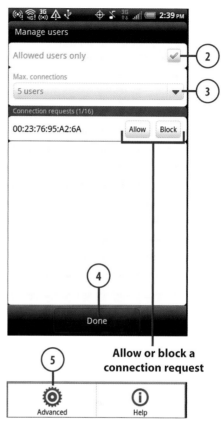

Allow or block a connection request

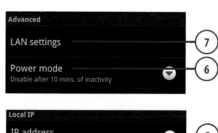

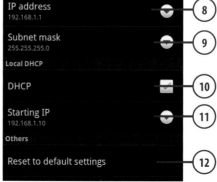

Add Gmail, POP3, IMAP, and Microsoft
Exchange mail accounts, as well as
work with mail settings

In this chapter, you learn how to use your EVO 3D's email applications for Gmail and other mail accounts such has POP3, IMAP, and Microsoft Exchange. Topics include the following:

→ Gmail
→ Setting up the mail application
→ Working with the mail application

6

Emailing

Your EVO 3D utilizes two different mail programs: Gmail and the Mail application, which lets you set up POP3, IMAP, and Microsoft Exchange accounts. Each program offers a variety of features for managing your email and customizing your accounts.

Gmail

Part of the process of activating your EVO 3D involves setting up a Gmail account. You have the convenience of setting up more than one Gmail account on your phone, which is handy if you need separate email accounts for work and for personal use.

Adding a Gmail Account

You set up a Gmail account during the activation of your EVO 3D. Follow these instructions to set up a second Gmail account.

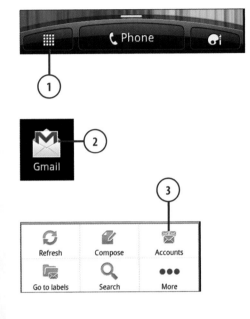

1. By default, the Gmail app is not on the EVO 3D Home screen. Tap the app icon on the Home screen to access the application menu.

2. Tap Gmail.

3. Touch the Menu button on your EVO 3D and then tap Accounts.

4. Tap Add Account.

5. Tap Google.

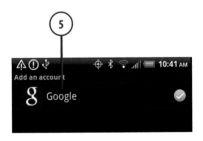

6. Tap Next.

7. Choose whether you want to create a new Gmail account or add a preexisting Gmail Account.

8. If you choose to add a preexisting Gmail account, enter the Username and the Password for the account.

9. Tap Sign In. Skip to step 23 if you already have a Gmail account.

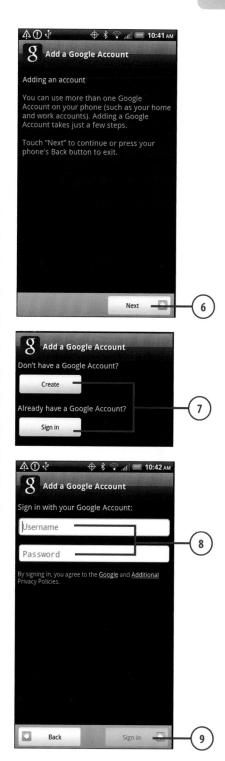

10. If you chose to create a new Gmail account, enter your first and last name.

11. Enter the Gmail address you would like to have and tap Next.

12. If the address you have entered is already taken by another Gmail user, a screen suggesting alternative addresses opens. Select an alternate address and then tap Next.

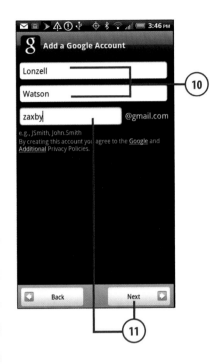

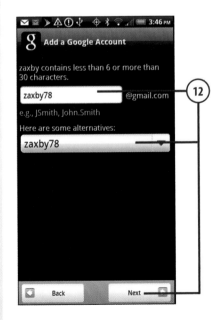

13. Enter a password for the new account.

14. Retype the password in the Confirm Password box.

15. Tap Next.

16. Select a security question.

17. Enter the answer.

18. Enter a secondary email. This should be an existing email account.

19. Tap Create.

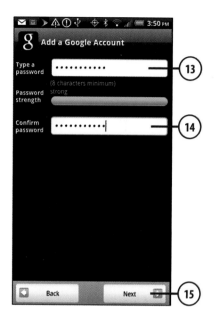

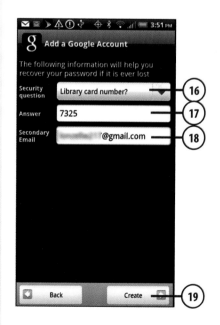

20. Read the Google Terms of Service and then tap I Agree, Next.

21. Enter the characters that match the CAPTCHA image.

22. Tap Next.

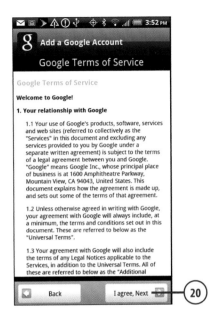

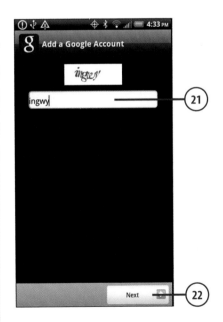

23. Select to synchronize to your EVO 3D.

24. Tap Sync Now.

25. Tap Finish Setup.

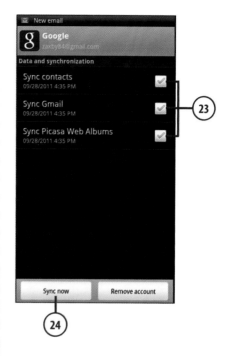

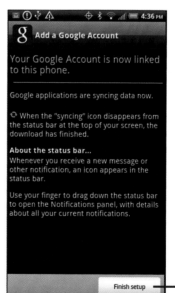

Composing Gmail Email

Now that you have set up your Gmail accounts, you are able to share and receive email using Gmail.

1. If you have more than one Gmail account, all accounts appear in a list when you tap the Gmail icon. Tap the account you want to use.

2. Press the Menu button and then select Compose.

3. Enter the recipient's email address in to the To field. If the recipient is in your contacts, begin typing his name to see matches from your Contacts and then touch the name.

4. Enter a subject.

5. Type your message.

6. If you want to add a photo as an attachment to the email, press the Menu button and then tap Attach.

Attaching 3D Photos and Video

If you tap a photo that is in 3D, you receive a message alerting you that you can use the photo as 3D or 2D. If the person does not have an EVO 3D phone, select to use the photo as 2D. As of this publication, you cannot select between 2D or 3D videos to attach to a message.

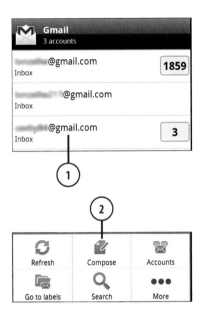

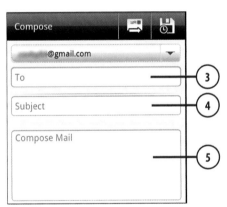

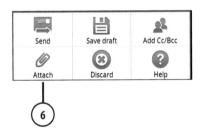

7. Tap the album that contains the picture you want to attach.

8. Tap the picture(s) that you want to attach. The image is attached to the email and you are taken back to the email message.

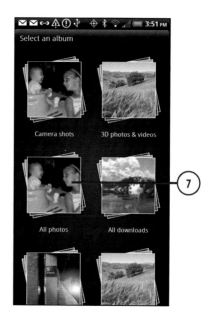

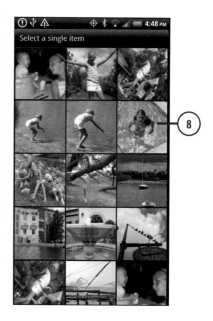

9. Press the Menu button again and then tap to save a draft of the email. You can also tap the icon in the upper-right corner that resembles a floppy disk.

10. Tap to send a carbon copy or blind carbon copy to another person. When you send a blind carbon copy, you can copy someone else without the main recipient knowing about it.

11. Tap to discard the message.

12. Tap to send the email.

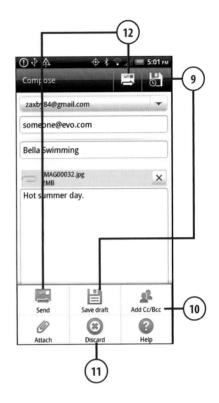

Reading Gmail Email

Obviously, reading your email is a very straightforward process. This section covers a few features that can help you get most from using Gmail on your EVO 3D.

1. Tap an email to open it.

2. Tap to add the sender to your Contacts. If the sender is already in your Contacts, you are given the options to place a call to the sender, view the sender's contact information, send a message, or email the sender.

3. Tap to add a star next to the email in your inbox, which serves as a reminder of something important within the email.

4. Tap the curved arrow to reply to the sender.

5. Tap the arrow tip to reveal the options to Reply All and Forward the email.

6. Tap to download the attachment to your phone.

7. Tap to preview the attachment without downloading it to your phone.

8. Tap to archive the email.

9. Tap to delete the email.

10. Tap to navigate to the previous email in the inbox.

11. Tap to navigate to the next email in the inbox.

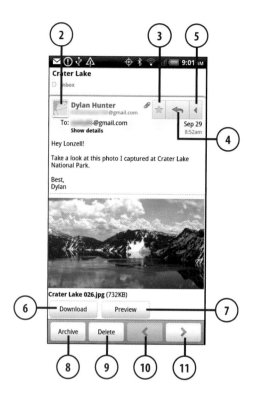

12. Press the Menu button to view more options. Tap to change labels. Labels are Gmail's name for folders.

13. Tap Mark Unread so that the email returns to unread status.

14. Tap Go to Inbox to view all the mail in your Gmail inbox.

15. Tap Mute to block email from this sender.

16. Tap to add a star next to the email in your inbox.

17. Tap More to view more options.

18. Tap to report this email as spam.

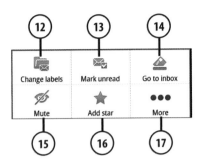

Report Spam

When you report a message as spam, that message is labeled as spam, and a copy of the email is sent to Gmail's Spam servers. When you make Gmail aware of a possible new spam email that is circulating, it can assess if similar emails have been received by other Gmail users and then block that spam from reaching other users. When you report possible spam, you are helping all Gmail users.

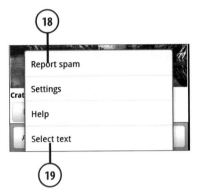

19. Tap Select Text to select text within an email.

20. Tap the text you want to select and drag the handles around the text you want to select.

21. Tap the highlighted text to copy it to the clipboard so that you can paste the text in a new location.

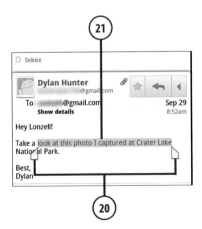

22. Touch and hold your finger where you want to paste the text and then select Paste from the menu that displays.

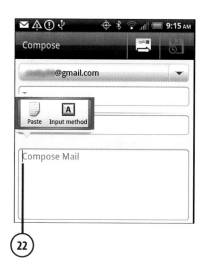

STARS AND LABELS

Stars and Labels are used by Gmail to help you organize your messages. With most email clients, you create folders to separate your emails by topic. For example, you could create a folder named Vacation Plans in which you store all of the emails from family, friends, and your travel agent regarding plans for your summer vacation. Gmail uses the term labels instead of folders. You can create a label named Vacation Plans and then choose email messages to place under that label. An email you mark with a star appears with a star next to it when you view the inbox. A star next to a message can help you remember that a particular email in your inbox holds some special significance.

>>> Go Further

Gmail Settings

Gmail provides a variety of settings for you to customize your email experience, including appending a signature to messages and configuring notification settings.

1. When you are within the Gmail app, press the Menu key and then tap More.

2. Tap Settings.

3. Tap to create an email signature.

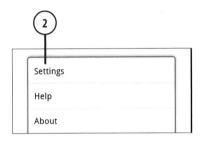

Email Signature

Gmail enables you to customize your own email signature, the same as you would in an email client on your Windows or Mac computer. You can add your own personal touch to the bottom of outgoing email messages in the form of a block of text displaying your contact information or a short quote. You can use your signature to sell yourself by listing your job title, degrees, certifications earned, or awards won.

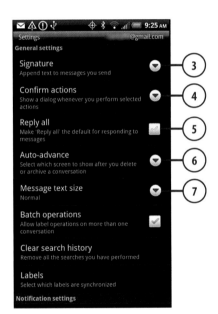

4. Tap Confirm Actions to enable or disable confirmations when you archive, delete, or send emails.

5. Tap to enable or disable Reply All as the default for responding to messages.

6. Tap Auto-Advance to select which screen shows after you delete or archive a conversation.

7. Tap to adjust the default font size of text.

8. Tap Batch Operations to enable or disable the ability to select more than one message when working with labels.

9. Tap to clear your search history.

10. Tap Labels to select which labels to synchronize.

11. Scroll down to reveal more options.

12. Tap to enable or disable the notification of email in the status bar.

13. Tap to select a ringtone for when you receive a message.

14. Tap to enable or disable vibration when you receive a message.

15. Tap to enable or disable whether you are notified once for a new email and not for every new message.

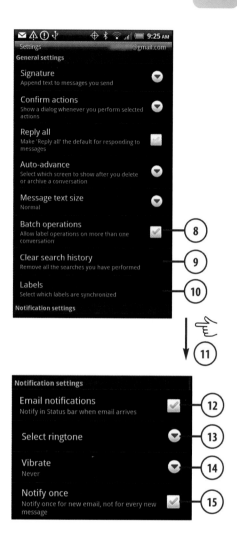

Setting Up the Mail Application

Along with the Gmail application, which only supports Gmail, the Mail application provided enables you to work with Microsoft Exchange, POP3, and IMAP email accounts. Online email hosts such as Hotmail and Yahoo! typically use POP3 and IMAP accounts, and Microsoft Exchange accounts are typically used by businesses. Generally, the mail application can set up new accounts automatically, but occasionally you have to perform a manual setup.

Adding a New Microsoft Exchange Account

If the EVO 3D is your only phone, it would be practical for you to add mail accounts for both personal and work use. You need to perform a manual setup to add a Microsoft Exchange account to your phone. You might need to speak with your network administrator to gather server and domain information before following these steps.

1. Tap the Mail application on the Home screen.

2. Tap Accounts List.

3. Select New Account.

4. Select Microsoft Exchange ActiveSync.

5. Enter your corporate email address.

6. Enter your network password.

7. Tap Manual Setup.

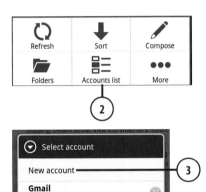

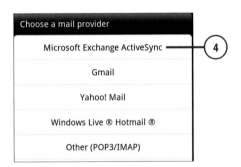

8. Type your corporate email address if it has not been carried over from the previous screen.

9. Type in the ActiveSync server address.

10. Type the corporate domain.

11. Type your username.

12. Type your corporate password if it has not been carried over from the previous screen.

13. Tap to enable or disable the use of SSL. This setting is usually enabled.

14. Tap Next.

15. Tap to enable or disable the synchronization of mail.

16. Tap to enable or disable the synchronization of your contacts. When you leave this setting enabled, your Outlook contacts sync to your EVO 3D.

17. Tap to enable or disable the synchronization of your calendar.

18. Tap to enable or disable this mail account to automatically check for new email in the corporate inbox and have it delivered to your phone.

19. Tap to change frequency in which email is delivered to your EVO 3D.

20. Tap to enable your phone to check your corporate inbox for new mail and deliver it to your phone, only after you access the Mail application.

21. Tap Next.

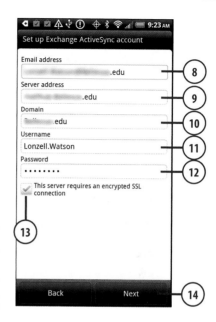

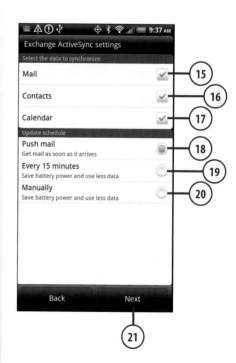

22. Type a name for this email account.

23. Tap Finish Setup.

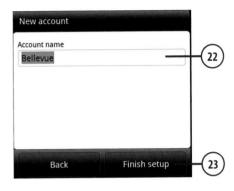

Exchange Account Settings

After you have set up your Microsoft Exchange account, you configure how that account functions on your EVO 3D.

1. From the Exchange inbox screen, press the Menu button and then tap More.

2. Tap Settings.

3. Tap Account Settings to edit the information you used to set up your Exchange account.

4. Tap General Settings to change settings including font size, signature, and default email account status. The General Settings screen opens.

5. Tap Font Size to change the default font size in messages for this account.

6. Tap to use a personal signature that displays at the bottom of each email you send.

7. Tap to personalize your email signature.

8. Tap to make this account your default email account. Your default email account is the account that mail will be sent from when you select a mailing option within another application or a website.

9. Tap Attachment Cache to select where to save email attachments.

10. Tap to enable or disable the display of a confirmation box when deleting an email message.

11. Tap to enable or disable the automatic refresh of an email folder when you open it. The default folder is the Inbox.

12. When you view messages from the Inbox screen, you can see a few lines of text beneath the subject. Tap to set the number of lines of text that displays for messages in the Inbox.

13. Press the Back button at the bottom of your EVO to return to the previous screen.

14. Tap Send and Receive to change server settings.

15. Tap to set the maximum email file size for incoming messages, which is 50KB.

16. Tap to set messages to display in HTML or plain text format. The default is HTML.

17. Tap to change the frequency with which to check for new messages.

18. Tap Download Past Mail to set how many days to download past messages.

19. Tap Include File Attachment to set the size of email attachments that will be automatically downloaded with email messages. By default, this is set to never automatically download attachments. For security issues, consider leaving this set to Never.

20. Tap to enable or disable email synchronization when roaming. To avoid expected roaming charges, consider leaving this setting disabled.

21. Tap Auto Download Message to enable or disable the automatic download of email messages as you scroll down the screen.

22. Tap to choose which folder to synchronize whenever you launch Mail. When you tap the Mail application, the folder you choose here updates. The default folder is the Inbox.

23. Tap to enable or disable if your reply email message includes the original receive mail.

24. Scroll down to view one more option.

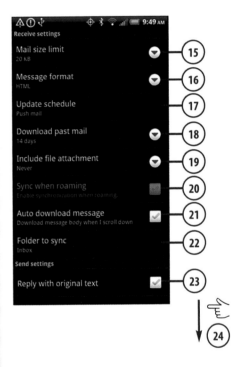

25. Tap to enable or disable whether you receive a copy of the messages you send.

26. Press the Back button at the bottom of your EVO 3D to return to the previous screen.

27. Tap to adjust email notifications settings such as sound and vibration.

28. Tap to remove this Microsoft Exchange account from your EVO 3D.

Adding a New POP3 or IMAP Account

POP3 and IMAP accounts are typically used by hosted email accounts such as Hotmail and Yahoo!. The EVO 3D usually does a good job automatically setting up accounts with common email providers, including large ISPs such as Comcast and Road Runner. An automatic set up might not work for smaller ISPs or if you have created your own website. If you need to manually set up your account, you need to obtain its server information. Check under the support section of your ISP or email your service provider's website for instructions on how to set up your email on a smartphone. Here is how you manually set up a POP3 or IMAP account on your EVO 3D.

1. Tap the Mail application.

2. While in the Mail Inbox, press the Menu button and then select Accounts List.

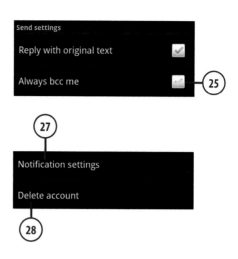

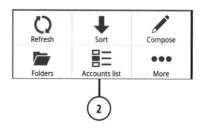

3. Tap New Account.

4. Tap Other (POP3/IMAP).

5. Enter your email account address.

6. Enter your email password.

7. Tap Manual Setup.

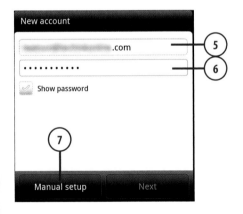

8. Tap to choose a protocol. Your choices are POP, APOP, IMAP.

APOP

APOP, Authenticated Post Office Protocol, is an extension of the Post Office Protocol (POP) in which your account password is sent in encrypted form. When you check your email with standard POP, the username and the password for your account is sent in plain text over the network, which can make it vulnerable to a malicious third party. The APOP encryption process makes it more difficult for your email to be hacked. APOP is a more dated method for mail authentication encryption.

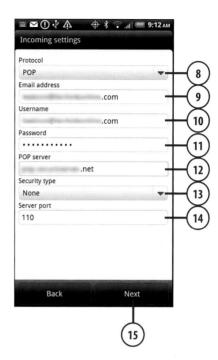

9. Type in your email address if it has not been carried over from the previous screen.

10. Type your username.

11. Type your password.

12. Enter the POP server, if necessary. A POP account was chosen, so a POP server was entered.

13. Tap to select a security type. Your choices are None, SSL, and TLS.

14. Change the incoming server port if necessary.

15. Tap Next.

16. Type your username if this information wasn't carried over from the previous screen.

17. Type your password if this information wasn't carried over from the previous screen.

18. Type the server name for outgoing mail.

19. Tap to select a security type. Your choices are None, SSL, and TLS.

20. Change the server port, if needed.

21. Tap Next.

Security Type

If your email provider supports SSL or TLS, you should use it; otherwise the mail you send and receive goes over the Internet in plain readable text. When you use SSL or TLS, your emails are encrypted as they travel.

22. Type a name for this email account.

23. Type your name.

24. Select to make this account your default email account. Your default email account is the account that mail will be sent from when you select a mailing option within another application or a website.

25. Tap Finish Setup.

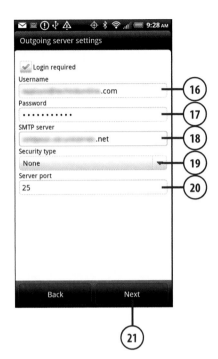

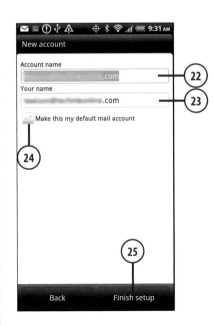

Working with the Mail Application

Now that you have set up multiple accounts with the Mail application, you are ready to send, receive, and manage your email messages. The instructions for using the Mail app are the same for each email account you have added.

Using Combined or Separate Inboxes

If you have a few email accounts on your phone, the Mail application makes it easy for you to check all of your email in one location. Instead of navigating to each individual account to check messages, you can check all your email accounts from a unified inbox.

1. While in an inbox, press the Menu button and then tap Accounts List.

2. Select an individual account to view only its inbox.

3. Select All Accounts to view messages from each email account inbox from one unified inbox. Up to 15 email accounts can be shown in the unified inbox.

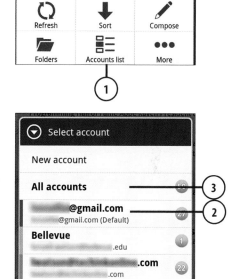

4. When viewing all inboxes, each message from a different inbox appears with a different color bar on the far left. In this example, orange represents the Exchange emails, blue represents POP3 messages, and red represents Gmail messages.

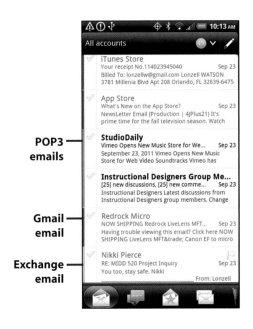

Navigating the Main Screen

The Mail app has multiple views you can access to help you manage your accounts and messages. You can switch between inboxes and also filter each inbox.

1. Tap to switch between different email accounts.

2. Tap to compose a message.

3. Tap an email to read it.

4. A grayed-out message indicates that it has already been read.

5. Bold font indicates that a message has not been read.

6. Tap the check marks to select multiple email messages and work with them as a group.

7. Indicates how many emails have not been read.

8. A paperclip indicates that a message has an attachment.

9. A red exclamation indicates an urgent email.

10. A red flag indicates that you have flagged the email.

Flag an Email Message

You can flag an email to serve as a reminder that there is something important within that message.

11. Tap to see the conversations view. This view is great if there has been a lot of back-and-forth for a particular email. You can view the entire conversation from this view.

12. Tap to view or edit messages you have marked as a Favorite.

13. Tap to see a list of all unread email for this account. Scroll to the right to see more options.

14. Tap to view a list of all emails you have flagged.

15. Tap to view all meeting invitations. Scroll to the right to see another option.

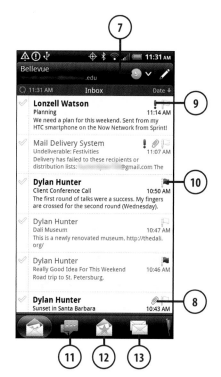

16. Tap to see a list of all emails that contain file attachments.

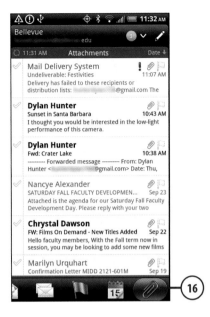

QUICKLY BROWSING THE INBOX

You can quickly navigate an inbox that has many messages by choosing a filter order and then using finger gestures. Press the Menu button and then select Sort to choose a sort order. The default sort order is Date (most recent). After choosing a sort order, place two fingers on any message in the Inbox and drag up and down the screen. The screen jumps to the set of email messages based on the sort order you have chosen. In this example, an overlay of dates appears on screen as you drag up and down, which can help you locate a message by date.

Composing Email

You can use the same steps for composing emails regardless of which email account you are in.

1. From an inbox, press the Menu button and then choose Compose. You can also tap the pencil icon to begin composing a new email.

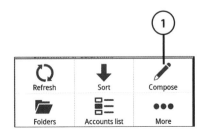

2. Type in the recipient's name, and if the name is in your Contacts, it appears in a list from which you can select it. The recipient's address appears under the To field. If the recipient is not in your Contacts, just complete typing the address and tap the Return button on the keyboard. Then type another name into the To field to send the message to multiple recipients who are not in your contacts.

3. Tap the icon that looks like a head and shoulders to select contacts to which you want to send the email. This is a quick way to select multiple contacts and then designate them simultaneously as recipients.

4. Touch and hold your finger to a recipient to edit recipient information, including removing a recipient and saving to an existing group.

5. Tap to enter a recipient to receive a carbon copy or blind carbon copy of the email.

6. Tap to edit the recipient information for the email.

7. Enter a subject for the email.

8. Enter the email message.

9. Tap to delete the email.

10. Tap to save a draft of the email.

11. Tap to send the email to the recipient(s).

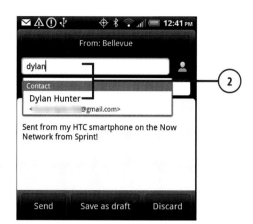

No Connection

If you send an email while your EVO 3D is not connected to a Wi-Fi network or data connection, or when it is in Airplane mode, your email is saved to the Outbox folder and is sent automatically the next time your phone syncs.

12. Press the Menu button to receive more options, some of which are redundant to the setting found on this screen.

13. Tap to give the current message a priority status.

14. Tap to add an attachment to the email.

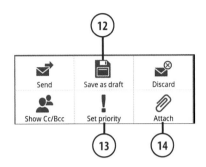

Reading Email

Of course, reading your email is a very straightforward process. This section covers a few features that can help you get the most from using the Mail app on your EVO 3D. Reading email in the Mail app is the same regardless of which email account you are in.

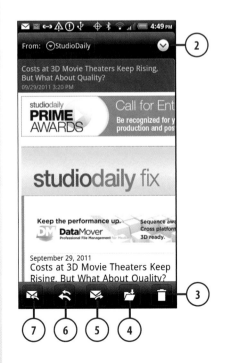

1. Tap an email to open it.

2. Tap to view all recipients of the email.

3. Tap to delete the current message.

4. Tap to archive the current message.

5. Tap to forward the current message to another person.

6. Tap to reply to the sender and all recipients of the message.

7. Tap to reply to only the sender of the message.

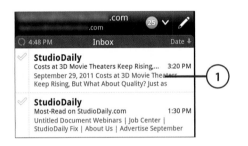

8. Press the Menu button for more options and then tap List to return to the current email account inbox.

9. Tap Previous to navigate to the previous email within the inbox.

10. Tap Next to navigate to the next email within the inbox.

11. Tap Mark Unread to return the message to an unread status.

12. Tap to see the conversations view. This view is great if there has been a lot of back and forth for a particular email. You can view the entire conversation from this view.

13. Tap to print the current email from a wireless printer that you have previously added to your EVO 3D. Both the printer and the device must be on the same network.

Get the most
from the Internet
using your EVO
3D browser

In this chapter, you explore the World Wide Web on your EVO 3D using your phone's web browsing features. Topics include the following:

→ Bookmarking websites
→ Sharing websites with others
→ Using GPS ability with web browsing
→ Keeping track of the websites you visit

Browsing the Web

Your EVO 3D offers great features for experiencing the Internet. The experience of using your EVO 3D's web browser is similar to using an Android tablet's web browser or even a desktop computer's browser—just with a smaller screen. You have many options for optimizing your web-browsing experience at your fingertips, and you also have the benefit of holding your EVO 3D in landscape orientation to increase your screen's viewing area.

Navigating with the Browser

Much like the browser on your desktop computer, you can customize your EVO 3D's browser, bookmark sites, and see a record of your browsing history. Your EVO's Home screens are already configured for you to access the browser with just a flick of your finger.

1. From a Home screen, tap the Applications icon.

2. Scroll down one screen and then tap Internet.

Perform a Quick Google Search

Flick the default Home screen from right to left to access a Google search field. This is much quicker than accessing it from within the Applications menu.

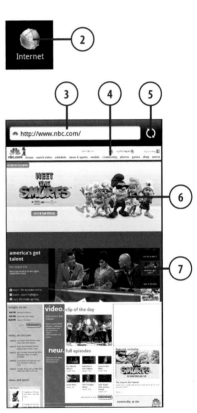

3. Tap to type in the address for the website you want to visit.

Hidden Address Field

When you access a web page, sometimes the browser moves the page up and conceals the address field. To access the address field again, simply pull the page down, and it shows up at the top of the page.

4. Tap a link to follow it.

5. Tap to refresh the page.

6. Double-tap an area on the page to zoom into that area. You can double-tap the area again to zoom out.

7. Unpinch your thumb and index finger to zoom into the web page. Pinch them together to zoom out.

8. Rotate your EVO 3D to view the web page in landscape orientation.

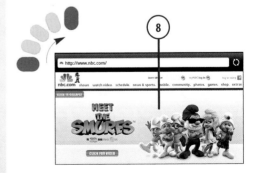

Managing Bookmarks

The browser makes it easy for you to save your favorite websites as book-marks so that you can quickly return to them later. Over time, you can accu-mulate a large number of bookmarks.

1. Press the Menu button on your EVO 3D and then tap Bookmarks. The bookmarks screen displays thumbnails of websites you have bookmarked. Your EVO 3D comes preloaded with some bookmarks to sites you might find useful.

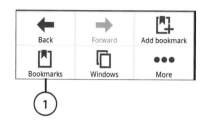

2. Tap a bookmark to load that web-site.

3. Press the Menu button and then touch Thumbnails to change the view of the Bookmarks screen from the default Grid view to a Thumbnails view or list view.

4. Touch and hold a bookmark to reveal the bookmark actions menu.

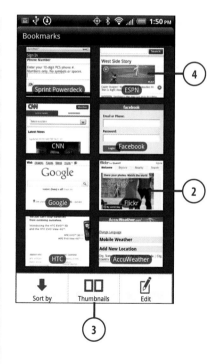

5. Tap to open the bookmark.

6. Tap to open the website in a new window.

7. Tap to edit the bookmark.

8. Tap to add a shortcut to the bookmark from your EVO 3D's Home screen. This enables you to access the bookmark without first having to open the browser.

9. Tap to share a link to a website with a friend via Bluetooth, Friend Stream, a mail account, messages, or Peep.

10. Tap to copy the link to the book-mark so you can then paste it into another browser.

11. Tap to delete the bookmark.

12. Tap to set the bookmark as your browser's Home screen, which is the page that opens when you first launch the browser.

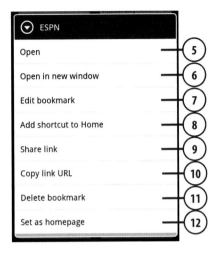

Friend Stream and Peep

The Friend Stream and Peep apps help connect you to your favorite social net-works. Friend Stream enables you to share and receive updates from friends on Facebook and Twitter in a single feed. Peep is a Twitter client that lets you post, read tweets, send and receive direct messages, and search for new Twitter users. You need a Facebook and Twitter account to use both Friend Stream and Peep. When you Tweet on your EVO using Peep, you can link your contacts to Twitter profiles with Twitter for HTC Sense. Both Twitter for HTC Sense and Peep share the same login credentials.

Using GPS Location

Your EVO 3D is equipped with a GPS radio that enables it to pinpoint exactly where you are. This function enables you to take advantage of the many loca-tion features included within many of the preloaded apps, third-party apps, and websites.

1. If you visit a website that wants to know your location, allow the website to update your location.

2. The Google Home page is used in this example. As you can see, the website is aware of my location and has given me options at the bottom of the screen to find restaurants, coffee, bars, and other services that are in my area.

Managing Multiple Windows

If you like to multitask, your EVO 3D makes it easy for you to open multiple web browser screens at the same time, load different web pages into them, and navigate between the multiple pages.

1. Press the Menu button and then touch Windows. The current page reduces to a thumbnail.

2. Tap to delete a page.

3. Tap a thumbnail of a page to display it in full screen again.

4. When you have multiple pages open, you can flick your finger left to right and vice versa to move through multiple open pages and tap a new page to view it full screen.

5. Tap to open a new browser. The new page opens in full screen.

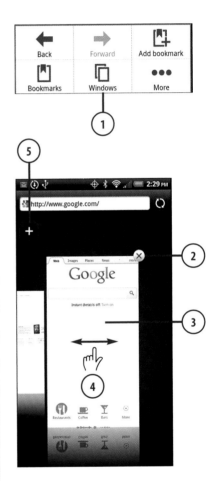

Setting Page Options

When viewing a web page, you have a number of options at your fingertips, such as performing a word search on a page, copying text, and sharing pages with others. You can find all of these options via the Menu button.

1. Press the Menu button and then tap More.

2. Tap Home to return to the first page that opens when you first launch the Internet.

3. Tap to perform a word search on the current open web page.

4. Tap to view the current page's address information.

5. Tap to share a page with others via Bluetooth, Friend Stream, mail accounts, Messages, or Peep.

6. Tap to view the Downloads queue for files you downloaded while using the browser.

7. Tap to review a comprehensive list of the sites you have visited using the browser.

8. Tap to wirelessly print the current web page. Both your printer and your phone must be connected to the same local wireless net-work.

9. Tap to customize the browser set-tings.

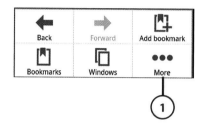

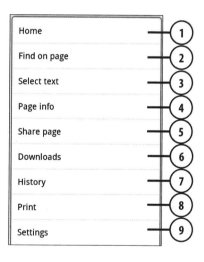

Customizing Browser Settings

There are many options for you choose from to customize how your browser behaves. For example, you can set a new Home page, decide whether images automatically load, and enable or disable mobile versions of web pages.

1. Press the Menu button and then tap More.

2. Tap Settings.

3. Tap to manually set a new browser Home page.

4. Tap Load Images to enable or disable image loading when you visit websites. When this setting is disabled, images do not load on the web pages you visit.

5. Tap to block pop-up window advertisements. It is a good idea to keep this setting enabled, as it keeps you from receiving unwanted solicitations. Some websites you visit might require you disable this setting.

6. Some websites offer mobile sites. Tap to disable this setting so that you can browse the full version of websites as if you were accessing them from a desktop computer.

7. Tap to enable or disable JavaScript. JavaScript is used on websites for formatting and other functions. Many web pages do not work without JavaScript, so consider leaving this setting enabled.

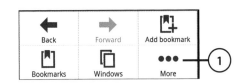

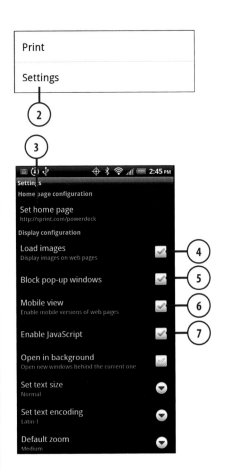

8. Tap so that the new web pages you open load in the background and do not become the current window. When you enable this setting, you have to switch to the new web page to make it the current window.

9. Tap to change the default text size for all web pages you visit. The default setting is normal, and your other choices are Tiny, Small, Large, and Huge.

10. Tap to set the text encoding to properly display text on web pages.

11. Tap to set the default zoom level for web pages on your EVO 3D. This setting ultimately determines how much of the physical webpage you are able to view onscreen at one time.

12. Scroll down to see more options.

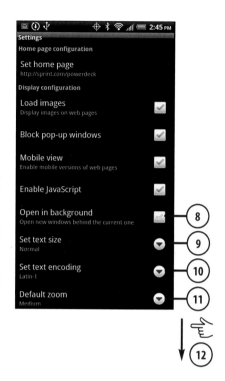

MOBILE BROWSING

Some websites can detect if you are browsing their sites using a mobile device and then direct you to mobile versions of the sites. A mobile version of a site usually means a stripped-down one. On occasion, some of the full website features you enjoy when browsing from your desktop computer might not be accessible in the mobile version. If you find that some of the mobile versions of websites you visit are too limiting, consider disabling this setting.

Go Further

13. Tap to display an overview of newly opened pages you visit. The web page appears zoomed out in an overview instead of it being viewed at 100%.

14. Tap Landscape-only Display so that all web pages viewed on your EVO 3D's web browser are displayed in landscape mode.

15. Tap Enable GIF Animation so that your EVO 3D is able to display GIF animations, which are animations composed of a number of images or frames displayed successively on a web page. Some individuals use GIF animations as their avatars in online forums.

16. Tap to clear all locally stored cookie data on your EVO 3D.

17. Tap to clear the browser cache.

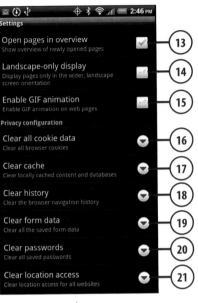

What's the Browser Cache?

The contents of the pages you have visited are stored in what is called the *browser cache*, which stores data and image information that enables websites to load faster when you return to them.

18. Tap to clear your browser history of all of the websites you have visited on your EVO 3D.

19. Tap to clear all previously entered web form data.

20. Tap to clear all data for passwords you have previously entered on websites.

21. Tap to clear all location settings for websites you have previously visited.

22. Scroll down to see more options.

How Form Data Is Saved

When you fill out an online form, by default that data is saved along with other browsing data on your phone. The browsing data includes user-specific information such as selections you made while filling out a form, shopping cart contents, and authentication data. Instead of deleting all categories of browsing data including browsing history, cookies, cache, and passwords, your EVO 3D enables you to pick specific items to delete, such as form data.

23. Tap to enable or disable your EVO 3D's browser from remembering the username and passwords you have entered on websites.

24. Tap Remember Form Data to enable or disable the browser's ability to remember form data such as name, address, and email address you have entered on websites.

25. Tap Show Security Warnings to enable or disable your browser from displaying a warning if there is a problem with a website's security.

26. Tap to enable or disable your browser from allowing websites to save and read cookies stored on your EVO 3D.

27. Tap to enable or disable your browser from allowing websites to access your location and GPS information.

28. Tap to set the amount of memory your EVO 3D uses for caching web content.

29. Tap to instruct your EVO 3D on how to use website plug-ins.

30. Tap to designate a new default search engine for your EVO 3D.

31. Scroll down to see more options.

32. Tap to configure advanced settings for individual websites you have visited, such as clearing location access for a specific website or clearing all data stored from a specific website on your phone.

33. Tap a website to view its settings.

34. Tap to disable this website's ability to see your location and GPS information.

35. Press the Back button to get back to the Settings menu.

36. Tap to enable Wi-Fi proxy settings and to set the Wi-Fi proxy host and the Wi-Fi proxy port.

37. Tap to reset your EVO 3D's browser back to its default state. This clears all the settings you have adjusted.

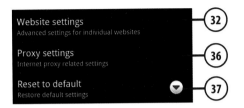

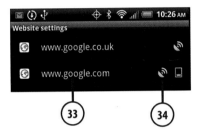

Downloading Files

While browsing websites, you might want to download video or audio files, documents, and perhaps even applications. Follow these steps to download files using your EVO 3D's browser.

1. Touch and hold a picture or a link for an object you want to download.

2. Tap Save Link.

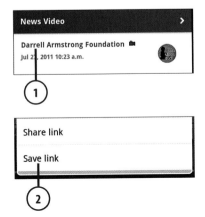

3. The Downloads screen appears with a progress bar for the download.

4. After the file has been downloaded, tap the file to view or play the content.

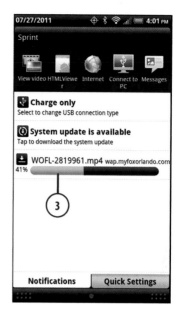

Reviewing History and Most Viewed Sites

Behind the scenes, your EVO 3D records the places you have visited on the Web. You can access these records within categories named Most Viewed and History.

Most Visited

Most Viewed is a list of websites that are ranked by how many times you have visited each site.

1. Open the browser, press the Menu button, and then tap Bookmarks.

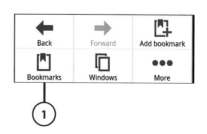

2. Tap to view a thumbnail list of your most-visited websites. All websites you have visited appear in the list with the most frequently visited site appearing first and so on.

3. Tap a website thumbnail to visit that site.

History

The History screen contains a record of all the sites you have visited. Each site is grouped by the date on which you visited it. The History screen offers a great way for you to find a site that you know you visited but did not make a note of the address.

1. Press the Menu button and then tap Bookmarks.

2. Tap to access your list of visited websites on the History screen.

3. Tap a category to expand the results and view the list of websites you visited on that day.

4. Tap a website name to visit that site.

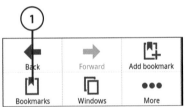

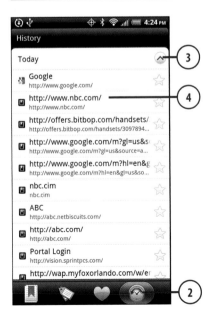

5. Press the Menu button and then tap Clear History to clear your browsing history.

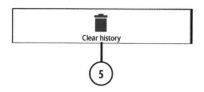

Use text and multimedia messaging to communicate with friends, family, and colleagues

In this chapter, you learn how to use text and multimedia messaging using the Messages app. Topics include the following:

→ Getting to know the messaging application settings
→ Creating text and multimedia messages
→ Attaching files to multimedia messages
→ Saving received attachments
→ Working with messages on your SIM card

8

Text and Multimedia Messaging

Text messaging, or what is referred to as Short Message Service (SMS) is perhaps the most widely used data application in the world, enabling you to converse back and forth, much like an instant messaging session. Multimedia Message Service (MMS) is a newer form of text messaging, providing you the ability to send photos, audio, and video in a message. Your EVO 3D is highly capable when it comes to text and multimedia messaging.

The Messaging Application

The Messages app on the Home screen is where you access the SMS and MMS capabilities of your EVO 3D. Within this application, you all you need to create and manage your messages and also tweak the application settings. Let's take a look at the application.

1. Tap Messages on the Home screen. The All Messages view opens, showing a list of all message threads. This page is empty if you have not sent or received any messages.

More Messaging Options

Press the Menu button on your EVO 3D while in the All Messages view to receive options to delete, compose, view message drafts, access settings, mark all messages as read, and send a group message. The options revealed by pressing the Menu button are contextual, meaning that depending on which screen you have up when you press the button, the options will be different.

Number of messages in thread

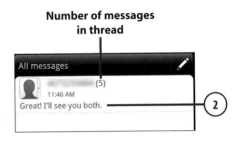

2. Tap a message to reveal all messages within a thread. The messages display back and forth text in a conversation between you and a recipient.

3. If the thread is long enough, you can flick your finger up and down to scroll through the conversation.

4. Tap an individual message to view the Message options.

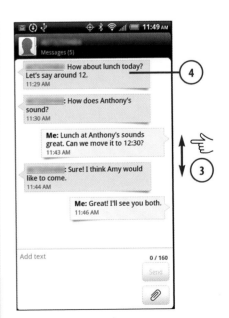

5. Tap Share to choose from a variety of delivery options in which you can share that message, including Bluetooth, a mail account, and Peep.

Peep This

Peep is a Twitter client that lets you post, read tweets, send and receive direct messages, and search for new Twitter users. You need to set up a Twitter account before you can use Peep. When you Tweet on your EVO using Peep, you can link your contacts to Twitter profiles with Twitter for HTC Sense. Both Twitter for HTC Sense and Peep share the same login credentials.

6. Tap Call to place a call to the sender.

7. Tap Save to People to add the sender's information into your contacts.

8. Tap to send a new message to the sender and start a new thread.

9. Tap Forward to forward the message to another person.

10. Tap View Message Details to view information about the message, including who the sender was and the date it was sent.

11. Tap Delete Message to delete the message.

12. Tap Lock Message so that the message cannot be deleted. A gray padlock appears in the message after you lock the message.

13. Press the Menu button on your EVO 3D to reveal more options. If the Messages options are up, you need to press the Menu button twice.

14. Tap All Messages to view all message strings on your EVO 3D.

15. Tap Quick Text to save time and take advantage of pretyped text replies such as: "I'm running late" and "In a meeting." Simply tap a pretyped message, and it is automatically placed within the message body.

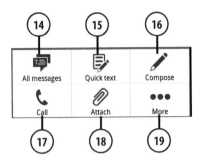

16. Tap Compose to create a new message.

17. Tap to place a call to the sender.

18. Tap to attach a file to a message.

19. Tap More for even more message options, such as Forward, Add Subject to add a subject line, Insert Smiley, Search, and more options.

Search Button

You can also tap the Search button on your EVO 3D to search for messages. When you hold your phone in Portrait orientation, it is the last button on the right at the bottom. The button looks like a magnifying glass.

Messaging Application Settings

You can manage how the Messages application manages incoming and outgoing messages from the Settings menu. Before you compose your first message, let's take a closer look at this application's settings.

1. From the main screen (the All Messages screen) press the Menu button and then tap Settings.

2. Tap Notifications to configure how your EVO 3D responds when you receive a message. Within the Notifications settings, you can decide whether or not to receive a visual or audible notification when messages are received, sent, or when a message cannot be sent.

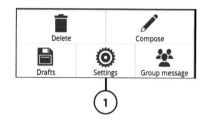

3. Tap Text Messages (SMS) to change the priority settings for messages from Normal to High, and to instruct your EVO 3D to support or not to support foreign accent characters. By default, your EVO 3D supports special accent characters.

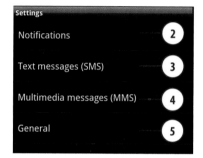

Changing the Priority Setting

A red exclamation mark appears within the message on your EVO 3D when you change the Priority setting from Normal to High.

4. Tap Multimedia Messages (MMS) to adjust the Auto-retrieve and Roaming auto-retrieve, Priority Level, Maximum Message Size, and Connection settings.

5. Tap General.

Don't Activate Roaming Auto-retrieve

It is best to leave the Roaming Auto-retrieve setting disabled when you travel to other countries because international carriers can charge large sums of money for using their networks. Consider calling Sprint before you travel to see if they offer an international SMS or MMS package for an up-front flat rate.

6. Tap to include the sent message history when searching for a message recipient.

7. Tap to include call history when searching for a message recipient.

8. Tap to include email addresses when searching for a message recipient.

9. Tap to select the number of lines of text that appear in a conversation on the All Messages screen.

10. Tap to instruct your EVO 3D to automatically delete older messages when the set limits are reached. Locked messages are not deleted. This option is used in conjunction with options shown in steps 11 and 12.

11. Tap Text Message Limit to choose the maximum number of messages to store in a conversation thread. This is with the exception of locked messages.

12. Tap Multimedia Message Limit to choose the maximum number of MMS messages to store in a conversation thread. This is also with the exception of locked messages. By default, your EVO is set to the maximum message size of 1 megabyte.

13. Tap to forward a text or MMS message to another phone.

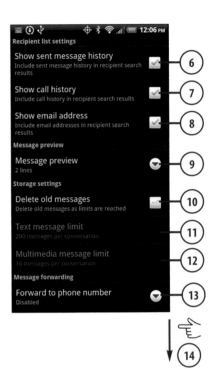

Possible Additional Charges

Forwarding could result in additional charges on your cellular bill. Be sure to contact Sprint for details before forwarding.

14. Scroll down to see more options.

15. Tap to forward a text or MMS message to another email address.

16. Tap this option to add a signature to all of your outgoing messages. This setting is used with the option found in step 17.

17. Tap to compose your own signature.

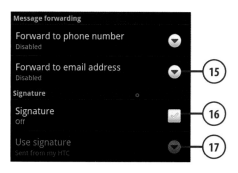

Composing Messages

You can compose a new message several different ways. You can tap the button that looks like a pen in the top-right corner of the All Messages screen, or you can press the Menu button and choose Compose from any screen within the Messages app.

1. Tap to compose a new message.

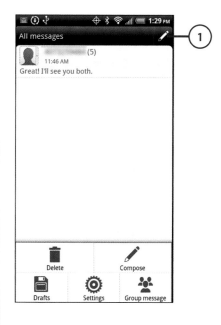

2. Type the phone number of the recipient. If the recipient is in your Contacts, type her name and then tap the name in the contacts results list or tap the Contacts icon to the right of the field and tap a name.

Hidden Contacts Icon

If you hold your EVO in the horizontal position while composing a new message, the Contacts icon does not appear to the right of the To field, as long as the keyboard is onscreen. You have to hide the keyboard to access this icon.

3. Tap and begin typing your message.

4. Press the Menu button on your EVO 3D and then tap More.

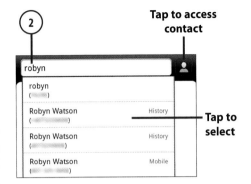

Tap to access contact

Tap to select

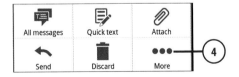

5. Tap Insert Smiley.

6. Select a Smiley.

7. Tap to speak your message.

Speaking Your Message

You can tap the button with a microphone on it, located on the keyboard, and then speak into your EVO 3D to let the Messages app dictate your message. Stop talking to end the message. You can even speak commas and periods to have them placed within the message.

8. Tap to send your message.

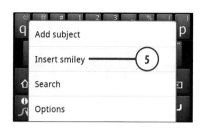

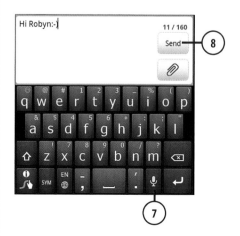

Attaching Files

The moment you add an attachment to an SMS (text message), your EVO 3D turns the message into an MMS (multimedia message). You can attach photos, video, and audio files.

1. After you type your message, but before you send the message, tap Attach.

Another Way to Attach a File

You can also press the Menu button on your EVO 3D while in the Messages app and then select Attach.

2. Tap Picture to view the options to take a picture with your EVO 3D and then attach the picture, or you can attach a picture already saved on your phone.

3. Tap Video to view the options to record a video with your EVO 3D and then attach the video or attach a pre-existing video that is on your phone.

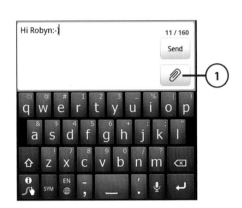

4. Tap Audio to view the options to record audio with your EVO 3D and then attach the audio file or attach a music file or sound that is already on your phone.

5. Tap Location to send a link to a Google map with your GPS coordinates.

6. Tap Contact to send a virtual business card complete with contact information. You are taken to your list of contacts.

7. Tap Appointment to share an existing appointment in your calendar with someone else.

Maximum Message Size
By default, your EVO 3D is set to the maximum message size of 1 megabyte.

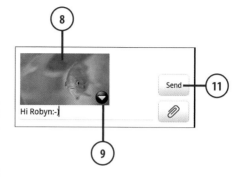

8. After you attach the file(s), you can see attachment(s) in the message. In this example, a picture from the Gallery was attached. Tap the attachment to view it in full screen.

9. Tap to access options that enable you to replace, remove, view in full screen, or change the duration of an attachment slide.

10. Tap the Back button to save the message as a draft.

11. Tap to send the message.

Receiving Messages

When you receive a text or multimedia message, you can read the message, view the attachment, and even save the attachment to your EVO 3D.

1. When you receive a message, you are notified with a ringtone. You also receive a new message alert on your EVO 3D screen. These notifications are also visible from the Lock screen.

2. Pull down the status bar and tap the new message to view it.

Another Way to Access Messages

When you receive a new message, you can also pull down the Notifications panel and then tap on a new message to open the app.

3. Tap the Play icon to view or listen to an attachment.

4. Tap to compose a reply.

5. Touch and hold a message to save or view an attachment in full screen.

6. Tap the phone number to place a call to the sender. If the sender is in your Contacts, his or her name appears here instead of their number.

Recipient and Sender Information Within a Message

If a person who is not in your list of contacts sends you a message, that person's telephone number appears within the message. If you receive or send a message from a person who is part of your contacts list, their name appears within the message. If you tap their name within the message, a list of actions appears, including the option to make a call.

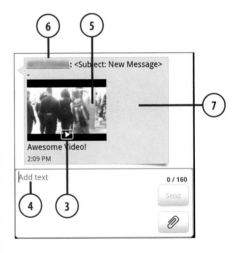

7. Tap in an empty area onscreen to access more message options.

8. If the sender has sent you multiple multimedia images, tap View Slideshow to view the attached images as a slideshow.

9. Tap to save a video to your EVO 3D.

10. Tap to place a call to the sender.

11. Tap to add the sender's information to your contacts.

12. Tap to send a new text message to the sender.

13. Tap to forward the message to a new recipient.

14. Tap to view the message details, including information such as date received, message class, and message size.

15. Tap to delete a message.

16. Tap to lock the message so it cannot be deleted.

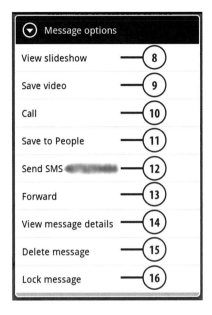

Delete Individual Messages versus Entire Threads

When you select Delete Message in the message options, you are only deleting one message, not the entire thread. To delete an entire thread, go to the All Messages screen and hold your finger down on it to access the Delete option for threads. You can also press the Menu button while on the All Messages screen to access the Delete option for threads.

Working with Messages

When you receive a text or multimedia message that also includes website addresses, email addresses, and phone numbers, your EVO 3D makes that text ready for you to use within the message.

1. If there is only one usable piece of text within the message, you can simply tap the message, and your EVO 3D takes the appropriate action. For example, if the message includes a link to a website, you can tap the message, and the website launches in the browser. If there are multiple linkable items within the message, simply tap the text to select that action.

2. Tap to place a call to the phone number listed in the message.

3. Tap to send an email to the address listed in the message.

4. Touch an open space in the message to access additional message options.

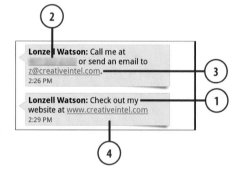

Use Date and Time, the Clock,
and Calendar apps to help
organize your daily events

In this chapter, you find out how to set the EVO 3D's date and time, use the Clock application, and use the Calendar app to help manage events. Topics include the following:

→ Synchronizing to the correct time
→ Using the Clock application
→ Setting Alarms
→ Working with the Calendar application

Date, Time, and Calendar

Your EVO 3D is highly capable of helping you manage a busy lifestyle. You can configure the date and time settings to automatically synchronize to the correct time, use the Clock application to set alarms, and manage appointments with the Calendar application. Managing multiple calendars is easy; the Calendar app synchronizes with your Google or Microsoft Exchange Calendars, so you are always up to date.

Setting the Date and Time

Before you begin using the Clock and Calendar apps on your EVO 3D, you want to make sure that your phone has the correct date and time.

1. Press the Menu button while on a Home screen and then tap Settings.

2. Scroll down and tap Date & Time.

3. Tap to enable or disable automatic synchronization of the date and time through Sprint. It is a good idea to leave this setting enabled because it synchronizes your phone wherever you travel.

4. Tap to set the date manually if you have disabled Automatic synchronization.

5. Tap to set the time zone manually if you have disabled Automatic synchronization.

6. Tap to set the time manually if you have disabled Automatic synchronization.

7. Tap to enable or disable the use of 24-hour time format. When you disable this option, time is no longer represented as a.m. or p.m. For example, 2:00 p.m. becomes 14:00.

8. Touch to change the format in which the date is represented. For example, the common format in the United States is 12/31/2011. You could change the format to 31/12/2011, which is normally accepted as the European date format. There are many other formats you can choose from under this setting.

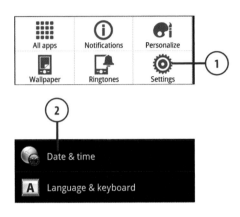

Navigating the Clock Application

The Clock application has a few more bells and whistles than just displaying the date, time, and weather. You can use the Clock app as a world clock, stopwatch, and countdown timer. This application can help you make sure you are always on time, no matter where you are.

Optional Desktop Dock

As of this publication, there is no official HTC dock accessory available for the EVO 3D, but there are some third-party docks for you to choose from. Generally, the dock serves two purposes: to charge your phone and to automatically launch the Clock application. Keep in mind that not all docks automatically launch the Clock application when you set the phone in the cradle, so do your research before purchasing a dock.

1. Tap Apps from a Home screen.

2. Tap Clock to launch the application.

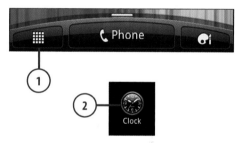

3. Tap to use the clock as a stopwatch. Notice that when you tap this icon, a new icon appears to the right of it in the shape of an hourglass.

4. Tap to use the clock as a timer.

5. Tap to use as an alarm clock.

6. Tap to use as a world clock.

7. Tap to return to the main Clock application screen.

8. Tap the weather information to access the Weather application and view forecasts for the next few days.

9. Tap to put the application in screensaver mode. When in screensaver mode, the date and time appear onscreen and change position every few minutes.

10. Tap to dim the desk clock screen. After the screen has dimmed, you can tap anywhere on screen to light up the screen again.

Signifies no alarm(s) set for the current day.

Managing Alarms

You can set multiple alarms within the Clock application and for one time only or to be reoccurring. By default, the alarms you set trigger even if you have your EVO 3D set to silent mode and have exited the Clock application.

1. Tap to manage alarms.

2. Tap to add a new alarm.

3. Tap to enable or disable an alarm. A green check mark appears in the box when an alarm is enabled.

4. Tap to edit a specific alarm. You can also use these three placeholder alarms to set a new alarm.

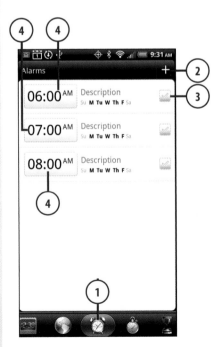

5. Press the Menu button and then tap Settings to change the overall alarm settings.

6. Tap to enable or disable if the alarms you have set are audible, even if you have your phone set to silent mode.

7. Tap to set the alarm volume.

8. Tap to set the duration of the snooze. Your options are between 5 and 30 minutes.

9. Tap to set how the side buttons on your phone respond when you press them while an alarm sounds. You have three choices: None, Snooze, and Dismiss. The default setting is Snooze.

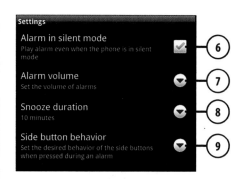

Adding and Editing an Alarm

The steps for adding and editing an alarm are the same. Both tasks are quick and easy to perform.

1. Tap the Add button or touch a specific alarm on the Alarms screen to make a change. The Set Alarm screen opens. This same screen opens if you had tapped a pre-existing alarm on the Alarms screen.

2. Drag up and down in the Hour, Minute, and AM/PM fields to set the time for the alarm.

3. Enter a description for the alarm.

4. Tap to choose an alarm sound for when the alarm triggers. You can choose from ringtones and music.

5. Tap to set the alarm to repeat. This setting is good when you only need to set the alarm for certain days, such as Monday through Friday and not the weekends.

6. Tap vibrate so that your EVO 3D also vibrates when the alarm triggers. This is a good setting if you happen to be in a loud environment when the alarm sounds.

7. Tap Done to accept the changes.

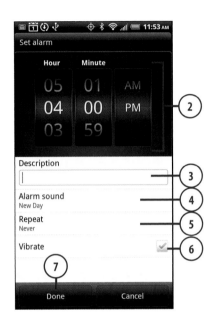

Viewing and Managing Weather

When you touch the weather symbol on the Clock application's Main screen, you can view hourly and five-day weather forecasts for the city you are in.

1. Tap the weather symbol.

2. The animation on this screen indicates the forecast for your current location. Tap to access more weather details from AccuWeather.com.

Indicates two forecasts have been added.

3. Tap to add a new forecast for a different location. When you add a new forecast, you can scroll through the different locations on this page by flicking up and down with your finger on the screen.

4. Tap to manually refresh the forecast.

5. Tap to return to the previous screen.

6. Tap Hourly to view the current forecast hour-by-hour.

7. Tap to view a five-day forecast.

Modifying Weather Settings

Inside the weather settings, you are able to set the forecast for a different location, tweak sync schedules, change the temperature scale, and enable sound effects. All you need to do is press the Menu button on your EVO 3D from a weather screen to access the settings.

1. Press Menu and then tap Refresh to manually update the forecast information.

2. Tap to view the edits you have made in the weather app, such as the addition of new location forecasts. This is the place to go to remove locations you no longer need.

3. Tap to add a new forecast location.

4. Tap to view a demo of the various weather animations that are preloaded on your EVO 3D.

5. Tap Settings to access the weather settings.

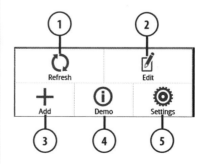

6. Tap to enable or disable the updating of forecast information upon opening Weather.

7. Tap to enable or disable if weather updates are synced automatically.

8. Tap to set the schedule for when weather information is synced automatically.

9. Tap to change the temperature scale between Fahrenheit and Celsius.

10. Tap to enable or disable sound effects for the Weather app.

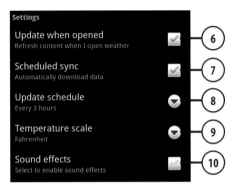

The Calendar Application

Your EVO 3D is equipped so that you are able to manage the important stuff, such as doctor appointments, business meetings, and anniversaries. You can view your calendar by day, week, month, or even as a list. You can see an overview of an entire month or a single day in detail. Any changes made within the Calendar app on your EVO 3D are automatically synchronized wirelessly to your Google Calendar.

>> Go Further

CALENDAR VIEW

There are five views in which you can view the contents of your calendar: Agenda, Day, Week, Month, and Meeting Invitations. When you first open the Calendar app, it launches in Agenda view, which provides a comprehensive view of scheduled events in one list. By default, Agenda view shows a limited range of scheduled events. You can instruct the Calendar app to show even more scheduled events on your phone and then flick the screen upward or downward to view the entire list.

The Day view is composed of a list of current events blocked for each hour. You can use your finger to flick up or down to scroll through the list. All events scheduled with the duration of All Day are located at the top of the list. You can flick the screen from right to left to jump ahead in increments of one day.

The Week view is arranged into seven parts with Sunday through Saturday at the top and the hours 12 a.m. to 11 p.m. on the left side. You can flick the screen from right to left to jump ahead in increments of one week.

Month view provides a broad view of events for a given month. Events scheduled for that month appear in a day box. The day box representing today is highlighted within the calendar. Any event designated as an All Day event is highlighted within the day box of the Month view.

The Meeting Invitations view displays all received meeting invitations for which you have not replied.

Navigating the Calendar App

Agenda view offers a great overall perspective for planning and assessing your calendar events one day at a time. The Agenda view displays events from the current day and into the next calendar year, including national holidays.

1. Tap Apps from a Home screen.

2. Tap Calendar. If this is your first time launching the Calendar app, it opens to the Agenda view. If you have launched Calendar before, it opens to the last view you accessed.

3. Events scheduled in your calendar appear in the list. You can also tap to show more events. Tap an event in the list to view information for that day's event.

4. Tap to view the calendar one day at a time.

5. Tap to view the calendar one week at a time.

6. Tap to view the calendar a month at a time.

7. Tap to view received meeting invitations to which you have not replied.

8. Tap to create a new event.

9. Tap to perform a search within the Calendar app.

10. If you have multiple calendars, tap to select a calendar in which to add your event.

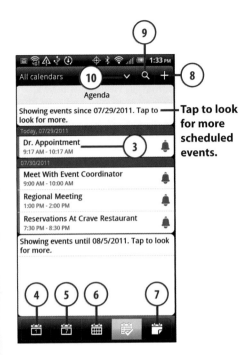

Tap to look for more scheduled events.

Adding a New Event or Appointment

Your EVO 3D is perfectly equipped for you to manage and create new events while on the go. The events you enter on your phone are automatically updated to your Google Calendar in real time.

1. Tap to view the calendar in Month view.

2. Tap to add a new event. Another way to create an event in Month view is to touch your finger to the desired day box and then choose New event from the menu that appears.

Indicates an appointment and approximately where in the day it is scheduled

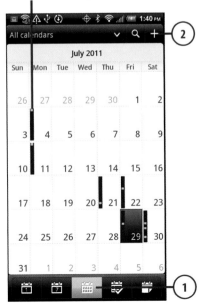

3. Tap to select which Calendar to add the event to. Choose PC Sync to create calendar events on your EVO 3D that you can sync with your computer's Outlook Calendar with HTC Sync.

4. Tap to enter the event's name.

5. Tap to enter the date the event starts.

6. Tap to enter the time the event starts.

7. Tap to enter the date the event ends.

8. Tap to enter the time the event ends.

9. Tap in the All Day check box to mark this event as lasting all day. When you mark an event as all day, the time start and end time fields become unavailable for you to adjust.

10. Scroll down to access more entry fields.

11. Tap to change the time zone.

12. Tap to review the new event in Day view.

13. Tap to enter the location for the event.

14. Tap to find the location you just entered on a map. This is a quick way to generate directions if you do not know how to find the location where the event is being held.

15. Tap to enter a description for the event.

16. Scroll down to access more entry fields.

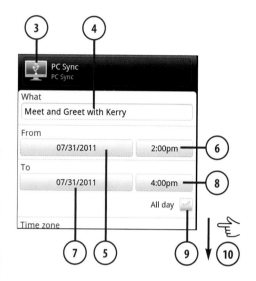

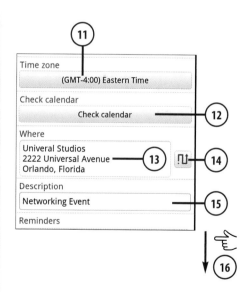

17. Set the minutes before an event that a reminder for the event should trigger.

18. Tap Repetition to set if this event repeats.

19. Tap Save to add the event to your calendar.

20. Tap Cancel to disregard this event entry form.

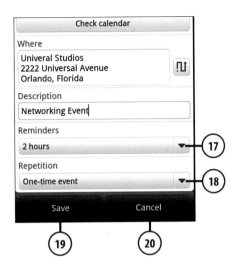

Editing or Deleting an Event

The details of your appointment, such as date and time, are always subject to change. Calendar makes it easy for you to update your appointment schedules so your information is always current.

1. Tap the event to open it.

2. Press the Menu button and then tap Edit Event to edit the information for that event.

3. Tap to delete the event.

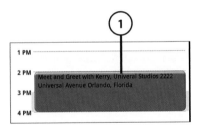

Another Way to Delete an Event

You can delete an event in Day, Agenda, and Week view by holding your finger on the event and then choosing Delete from the menu that appears.

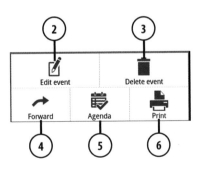

4. Tap to forward the event via Bluetooth, Mail account, or message.

5. Tap to view events as a comprehensive list of all events on your EVO 3D.

6. Tap to print the event details.

Deleting an Event Invitation

When you delete an event invitation that someone sent you, an event decline notice is automatically sent to the event organizer.

Responding to Event Reminders

After an event reminder has triggered, you can choose to snooze or dismiss the reminder.

1. After you have received a reminder in the notification bar, pull down the notification panel and tap the event reminder.

2. Tap to snooze the event reminders for five minutes.

3. Tap to dismiss all event reminders.

4. Tap to view the event details.

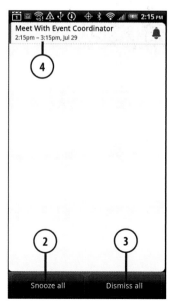

Calendar Settings

You can fine-tune the behaviors of the Calendar application, as well as designate which calendars to synchronize information with in the Calendar settings.

1. Press the Menu button from one of the five main Calendar views and then tap Settings.

2. Tap to use the same event reminder settings for all of your calendars. If you disable this setting, you can set different reminder settings for each calendar. After you disable this setting, new options that enable you to tweak each calendar's settings appear under this option.

3. Tap to choose how soon before an event you want to receive a reminder.

4. Tap to select the default reminder time before an event.

5. Tap to assign a sound to notifications.

6. Tap to show or hide events that you have declined.

7. Tap to change the default view in which Calendar opens.

8. Tap to choose the starting day of the week for month and week views. Your choice is Sunday or Monday.

9. Tap to include weather information in the day view event list.

10. By default, day view displays your current location's weather conditions. Tap to change to weather information for another location or city.

Responding to an Event Invitation

When someone sends you an event invitation, there are two ways you can respond. You can choose to respond from within your Gmail account or within the Calendar application on your EVO 3D.

Respond to an Invitation in Gmail

When you receive an invite, it appears within your Gmail inbox with the specifics for that event.

1. Open the invite in your Gmail inbox.

2. Tap Yes, Maybe, or No to specify if you plan to attend the event.

Respond to an Invitation in Calendar

When someone sends you an event invitation, it automatically appears in your calendar. The event appears in your calendar even if you have yet to accept the invitation.

1. Launch the Calendar app and locate the new event. Tap to open the event details.

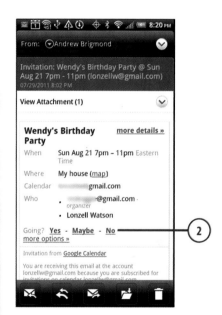

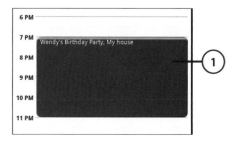

2. Tap Undecided.

3. Select a response to specify if you plan to attend the event.

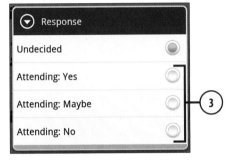

Capture photos with
Camera; store and view
photos with Gallery

In this chapter, you learn how to capture photos and videos; and manage your images and share them with friends and family. Topics include the following:

- → Using the camera
- → Viewing and managing your photos
- → Synchronizing photos with your computer
- → Working with doubleTwist

Capturing, Storing, and Viewing Photos

Along with transferring images from your computer to your EVO 3D, your phone is capable of capturing high quality photos and video, and you can literally house thousands of images organized in categories. The amazing thing about the EVO 3D is that it is also capable of 3D HD Imaging using the two 5-megapixel cameras located on the back of the phone.

Your EVO 3D's high-resolution, stereoscopic screen offers a great way to showcase photos and videos to friends and family without the use of special glasses. You can use Gallery to manage your images, perform basic edits, and even share your images via Bluetooth, Gmail, Messages, YouTube, and even more options.

Using the Camera

Your EVO 3D uses a pair of 5-megapixel, auto-focusing, rear-facing cameras located on the back of the device to capture photos or video in 3D or 2D. The EVO 3D is also equipped with a 1.3 megapixel front-facing camera, so you can video chat or take a photo of yourself. Both Photo and Video modes come with a unique group of settings to help you capture the best image.

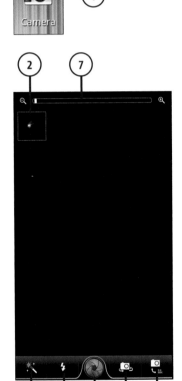

1. Tap the Camera application on the Home screen. By default your EVO opens in 2D photo mode.

2. Tap to preview your photos within the Gallery application.

3. Tap to place into video mode.

4. Tap to switch between rear-facing and front-facing cameras.

5. Tap to choose from a list of in-camera effects before you capture a photo.

6. Tap to deactivate the Flash feature.

7. Drag the Zoom slider to enlarge the framed scene. Be wary of this setting because it degrades the image.

8. Tap to take a picture. When you first touch the shutter button to take a picture, your EVO 3D first focuses the shot, and then when you remove your finger, the picture is captured.

The EVO 3D's Physical Camera Button

You can use the physical camera button located next to the 2D 3D switch on the EVO 3D to initiate capturing a photo or recording a video. In Photo mode, the physical button has two positions, halfway pressed and fully pressed. When you press the button gently, halfway down, the camera obtains a focus on the scene, you hear two beeps, and a green box appears onscreen. When you fully press the button, the actual photo is taken.

Tap Onscreen to Focus

You have the ability to selectively focus on one area within a scene you are capturing, with just a tap of your finger. Simply frame the scene and then tap the area you want on the display. The EVO 3D not only focuses on that area, but also adjusts the exposure of the scene for that spot. For example, when shooting a landscape that includes a skyline, try tapping the sky instead of the land so that you don't overexpose the sky. The same is true for when you are recording video with your EVO 3D.

Go Further

ADDING IN-CAMERA EFFECTS

Keep in mind when you use any of the photo or video effects, they become a permanent part of your pictures. To give yourself more choices in the future as to how you will use your images, consider adding effects after you take the photo using the effects options in the Gallery app or by purchasing an Android photo-editing program that enables you to perform such effects after you take the image. This way, you will be able to retain the unprocessed image for more flexible use in the future.

It's Not All Good

Digital Zoom Quality

Your phone has the ability to zoom, but be wary. The EVO 3D uses a 5x digital zoom that simply enlarges a portion of the image, simulating an optical zoom, thereby degrading the image. Moving physically closer, when possible, helps get you the highest quality image possible.

Changing Photo Settings

There are more settings you can adjust
that enable you to configure the
Camera app before you capture a
photo. Taking a photo can be as simple
as choosing a subject, composing your
shot, and pressing a button. The EVO
3D is also equipped with some very
helpful features commonly found on
dedicated photo cameras, including
manual exposure, white balance, flash,
and ISO settings.

1. From the Camera screen, press the
   Menu button, and then tap self-
   timer so that you can set a time
   delay before the camera automatically takes a photo. This enables
   you to put yourself into the scene
   before you capture the shot.

2. Tap to access slide controls that
   enable you to adjust the Exposure,
   Contrast, Saturation, and Sharpness
   of scenes before you take a picture.

3. Tap to change the white balance so
   that the camera can capture colors
   more accurately in different lighting environments. The Auto setting
   works well in most lighting situations.

4. Tap to choose an ISO level or set it
   back to Auto. The ISO settings enable
   you to adjust the camera's sensitivity
   to light. Use a higher ISO setting for
   low light shots, but beware of
   increased noise in the image.

5. Tap to select a default photo resolution to use.

6. Scroll down to view more options.

7. After you take a picture, your EVO 3D automatically lets you review the photo you have just captured, and then returns you to the viewfinder screen. Tap this setting to set the time for a captured photo to be displayed on the review screen before the screen changes back to the viewfinder.

8. Tap to select or deselect if photo resolutions are in 5:3 ratio, allowing you to frame the subject in the Viewfinder using the entire screen. When this setting is deselected, photo resolutions are in standard 4:3 ratio.

9. Tap to record GPS information into pictures. Embedded GPS information can come in handy if you use a photo-editing and managing application, such as iPhoto '09 and '11, that can use the location information to manage and showcase photos.

10. Tap to enable or disable if Camera will automatically reduce noise when using a high ISO setting and to automatically adjust picture brightness.

11. When you frame a scene using the Viewfinder, your EVO 3D automatically focuses on what is in the center of the screen. Tap to enable or disable centered autofocus. This is a good setting to leave enabled because you can always tap another area on screen to focus on a new area.

12. Scroll down to view more options.

13. Tap to enable Face Detection so that the camera automatically recognizes faces and adjusts the focus when you capture pictures of people. This setting is deactivated when you disable Auto Focus.

14. Tap to enable or disable the sound Camera makes when you take a picture.

15. Tap to display or not to display a grid on the viewfinder that makes it easier for you to frame and center subjects before taking a picture.

16. Tap to reset all settings to their original factory default states.

Viewing and Managing Your Photos

Gallery offers a photo and video management system that also allows you to view, capture, and perform basic edits on pictures. You can also share your photos from Gallery, play your media on a TV screen, or print photos right from your phone.

Gallery

By default, the Gallery application icon is not located on any of the seven EVO 3D home screens. You need to tap the Apps icon on the Home screen to access the widget.

1. Tap to launch the Gallery application.

2. Drag your finger up and down to see all photo albums.

Show/Hide Albums

Press the Menu button when viewing all albums to show/hide albums displayed on this screen.

Cannot Create a New Album

You can only edit, delete, and share a photo album from your EVO 3D. Unfortunately, you cannot create a new album from your phone. You need to create a new album on your computer and then sync it to your EVO 3D.

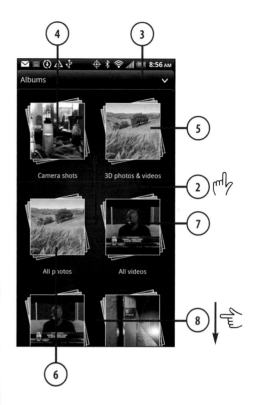

3. Tap to view and add albums from different accounts including Facebook and Flickr.

4. Tap the Camera shots album to view all photos and videos captured with your EVO 3D.

5. Tap the 3D Photos & Videos album to view only 3D photos and videos on your EVO 3D. This album contains some cool, preloaded 3D pics.

6. Tap All Photos to view all 3D and 2D photos on your EVO 3D.

7. Tap to view only videos.

8. Scroll down to view more albums.

9. Tap to view all photos and videos you have downloaded.

10. Tap to view some cool Sample 2D photos.

11. Tap to view some cool Sample 3D photos.

12. Tap to view any screenshots you have taken with your EVO. You need third-party software to capture screenshots on your EVO 3D.

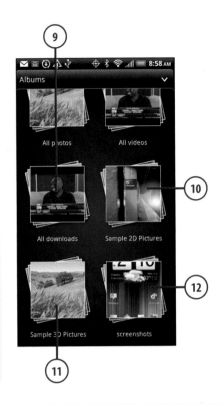

TAKING SCREENSHOTS

The EVO 3D requires a little help from the Android Software Developer's Kit (SDK) for you to take screenshots on your device. The Dalvik Debug Monitor Server (DDMS), which is part of the Android SDK, enables you to stage the screenshot and then capture the shot from your computer. There are a number of options available for taking screenshots on your EVO 3D. Some methods void your warranty, so make sure you do your research. The DDMS is free and does not void your warranty. You can download the Android SDK and access more information at http://developer.android.com/sdk/index.html.

Album Menus

After you open an album, you can easily delete, showcase, and share photos.

1. Tap a photo thumbnail to open an album.

2. Tap the Camera icon to launch the Camera application.

3. Tap the Trashcan icon to delete photos within the album. You are taken to another screen where you tap the photos you want to delete. An x appears over the photos you select, and then you can tap the Delete option at the bottom of the screen.

4. Tap to play a slide show of the photos within the album.

5. Tap to access options for sharing your photos such as via Bluetooth, Facebook for HTC Sense, Flickr, Gmail, and Mail.

6. Tap to view all albums on your EVO 3D.

7. Touch and hold your finger on a picture to view a list of options for that picture.

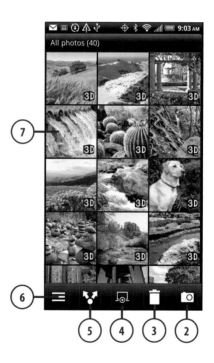

8. Tap to view the picture full screen.

9. Tap to access editing options for the picture.

10. Tap to share your photos via Bluetooth, Facebook, Flickr, Gmail, Mail, and more options.

11. Tap to set the picture as a Contact icon, Favorite, Footprints, and Wallpaper.

12. Tap to delete the picture.

13. Tap to start a slideshow of the entire album contents.

14. Tap to print the photo to a wireless printer.

15. Tap to review picture details including the date it was captured, file size, and photo resolution.

Managing and Sharing Photos in an Album

When you tap on a picture within an album to open it full screen, you can access more options for capturing new photos, editing photos, as well as sharing and deleting photos.

1. Swipe left and right to navigate through each picture within the album.

2. Tap the camera icon to launch the Camera application.

3. Tap the Trashcan icon to delete photos within the album. You are taken to another screen where you tap the photos you want to delete.

4. Tap to access options for sharing your photos.

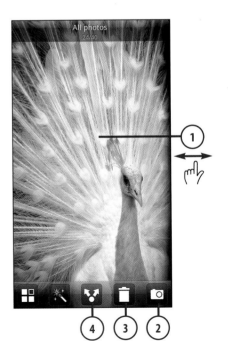

5. Tap to send this picture to another device using Bluetooth.

6. Tap to upload a photo to Facebook.

7. Tap to upload the picture to your Flickr account.

8. Tap to send the picture via Gmail.

9. Tap to send the picture using another email account (POP3/IMAP).

10. Tap to share the picture via the Messages app.

11. Tap to share the picture using your Twitter account.

12. Tap to share photos on the Picasa photo site.

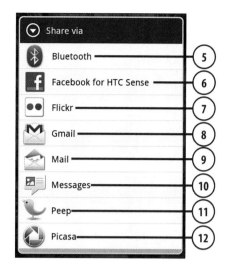

Editing Photos

After you open a photo and then tap the Edit button, you can perform edits such as cropping, rotating right or left, adding effects, and even adjusting 3D alignment of pictures.

1. Touch and hold your finger to edit the open picture. 3D photos have two more editing options than 2D photos, which are 3D-specific.

2. Tap to save a picture you captured in 3D in 2D. This comes in
handy if you want to share a picture with someone who does not
own an EVO 3D phone. If you
don't change the picture to 2D
before sharing it, the recipient
may not be able to view the
image file.

3. The cameras on the back of your
EVO 3D captures images at slight-
ly different angles, enabling your
phone to create 3D images. If
your 3D pictures are not aligning
well, causing you to strain your
eyes, tap here to adjust the alignment of the two images.

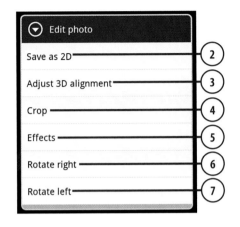

Aligning 3D Pictures

Keep in mind that it is not possible to
align each image perfectly, so the key is to
find the focus point of the 3D image and
align both images to that point. If you do
this successfully, your photographs
appear sharper, and your eyes experience
less strain when viewing them.

4. Tap to crop the image. Consider
cropping images to help define
the main subject in the picture.

5. Tap to add an effect to an existing
picture. When you add an effect
to a photo, the effect is added to
a copy of the photo and not the
original photo. If you add an
effect to a 3D image, the image is
converted to 2D to apply the
effect.

6. Tap to rotate an image to the
right.

7. Tap to rotate an image to the left.

Cropping Pictures

You can improve some photos by reframing the composition of the shot to remove unwanted areas. Fortunately, Gallery makes it easy for you to crop your EVO 3D photos. Cropping is a great way to correct shot composition and can help focus and emphasize the main subject of a shot.

1. Tap the Edit button.

2. Tap Crop to access the crop tool.

3. Touch and move the green crop tool to adjust where the image should be cropped.

4. Tap Save to save the cropped image. The newly cropped picture does not overwrite the original image but is saved as a copy within the album.

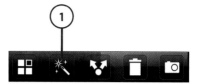

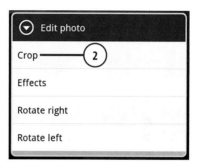

Printing Pictures

The Gallery application enables you to print your pictures to a Bluetooth-supported printer. You can print a picture by opening an album or reviewing a picture full screen and then pressing the Menu button on your EVO 3D to access the Print option. Before you can print, you need to have already paired your EVO 3D to the Bluetooth-enabled printer. Please refer to the "Connecting to Bluetooth Devices" section in Chapter 5, "Connecting to Bluetooth, Wi-Fi, and VPNs," for more information on wireless devices.

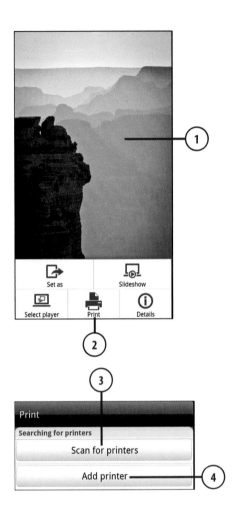

1. Open the photo that you want to print and then press the Menu button.

2. Tap Print.

3. Tap to scan for available Bluetooth-enabled printers.

4. Tap to add a new printer.

Synchronizing Photos with Your Computer

You can share photo collections you have on your computer with your EVO 3D by connecting your phone as an external drive or by using software such as doubleTwist. If you have not installed doubleTwist, please follow the directions in Chapter 1, "Getting to Know Your EVO 3D."

Connect as a Disk Drive

When you connect your EVO 3D to your computer, you can choose a connection type that allows your phone to charge only or to connect as a disk drive.

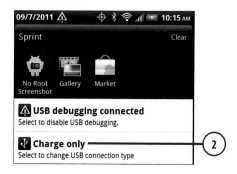

1. Connect your EVO 3D to your computer using the USB cable. The connection type screen is accessible, but you have to unlock your phone to see it.

2. Slide to unlock your phone, and then choose to connect as a disk drive. If you waited too long to make a choice on the connection screen, the screen disappears, but you can pull down the Notification panel and then tap the default Charge Only setting to reset the connection type.

3. Tap the Disk Drive option.

4. Tap Done to connect to your computer.

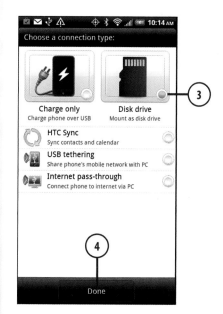

Moving Pictures (Mac OSX)

When you connect your EVO 3D to your Mac as a disk drive, you can drag and drop files to and from your phone like any other external storage device.

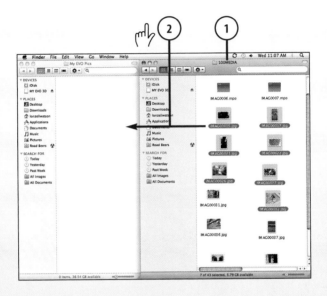

1. Browse your EVO 3D on your desktop and locate the pictures. You can find all pictures taken by your phone in DCIM\100MEDIA.

3D Files Cannot Be Opened

The 3D photo (.mpo) files are not recognizable on your desktop. Save pictures you have captured in 3D in 2D, within Gallery, before transferring them to your computer.

---

2. Drag the pictures that you want to move from your EVO 3D to your Mac.

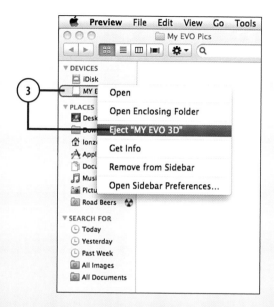

3. When you are finished, right-click the drive and choose Eject. If you don't eject your
    EVO 3D properly, you could damage the contents of your phone.

Moving Pictures (Windows)

When you connect your EVO 3D to your Windows computer as a disk drive, you can
browse and drag and drop files to and from your phone like any other external storage
device.

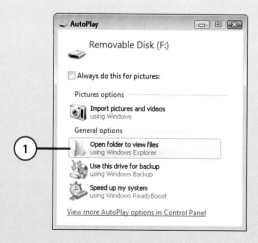

1. When the AutoPlay window opens, click Open Folder to View Files.

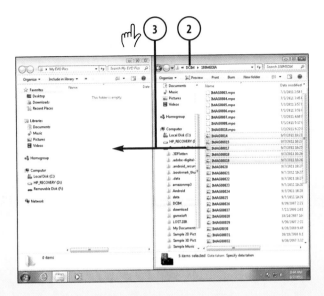

2. Browse your EVO 3D and locate the pictures. You can find all pictures taken by your phone or transferred in DCIM\100MEDIA.

3. Drag the pictures that you want to move from your EVO 3D to your Windows computer.

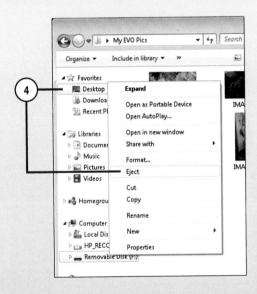

4. When you are finished, right-click the drive and choose Eject. If you don't eject your EVO 3D properly, you could damage the contents of your phone.

Working with doubleTwist

doubleTwist is a free desktop program that enables you to synchronize media to your EVO 3D. If you have not installed doubleTwist on your Mac or PC, please refer to Chapter 1 for instructions.

Transfer Photos Using doubleTwist

You can follow these steps for both Mac and Windows computers to transfer your photographs using doubleTwist.

1. Connect and mount your EVO 3D so that it appears under Devices in doubleTwist.

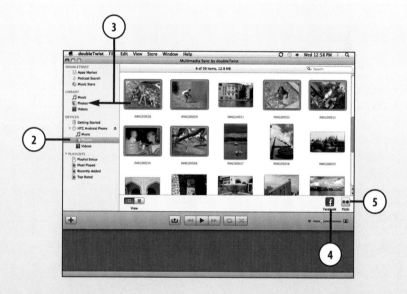

2. Click Photos under Devices.

3. Drag the pictures you want to move from your EVO 3D to the Photos folder in the doubleTwist library. The pictures are stored on your computer in a folder called doubleTwist within the Pictures folder.

4. Click to send one or more pictures to your Facebook account.

5. Click to send one or more pictures to your Flickr account.

6. Click to copy pictures from your doubleTwist library to your EVO 3D and then drag one or more pictures to Photos on your EVO 3D.

Configure doubleTwist Photo Options (Mac OSX)

You can configure the doubleTwist photo library to show one or more folders where you normally store folders, other than just the default folders. You can also exclude folders from showing in the library.

1. Click doubleTwist and then click Preferences.

2. Click Library.

3. Click to add new folders.

4. Click to Exclude folders.

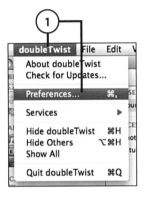

Configure doubleTwist Photo Options (Windows)

You can configure the doubleTwist photo library to show one or more folders where you normally store folders, other than just the default folders.

1. Click Edit and then click Preferences.

2. Select the Library tab.

3. Click a Folder button to add a new folder.

4. Click OK to save.

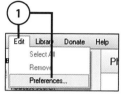

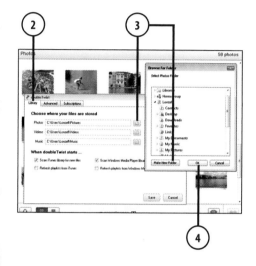

Search Android Market for thousands of productive, educational, and entertaining apps

In this chapter, you discover how to expand the capabilities of the EVO 3D by installing new apps. You also learn how to browse and make purchases on Android Market as well as manage application icons on your EVO 3D. Topics include the following:

11

- → Configuring Google Checkout
- → Navigating Android Market
- → Browsing apps by category
- → Deleting applications
- → Keep applications up to date

Enhancing Your EVO 3D with Apps

The EVO 3D is not just about state-of-the-art hardware craftsmanship. Your phone's true strength is in the incredible software that is developed for it. The HTC EVO 3D comes with some truly amazing, preinstalled apps right out of the box, but you can expand its capabilities even further by downloading new apps from the Android Market. You can choose from thousands of innovative apps, ranging from games to productivity apps.

Configuring Google Checkout

Before you can purchase app content on the Android Market, you first need to set up a Google Checkout account. You can choose to set up an account by going to the Google Checkout website on your computer, or you can add your information on your phone when you attempt to make a purchase for the first time. This process involves some typing, so consider setting up your account from your computer with the comfort of a full-size keyboard.

Downloading Free Applications

You don't need to create a Google Checkout account to download free apps from Android Market.

1. On your desktop computer, open a web browser and go to http://checkout.google.com.

2. Sign in using the Google account you used to set up your EVO 3D.

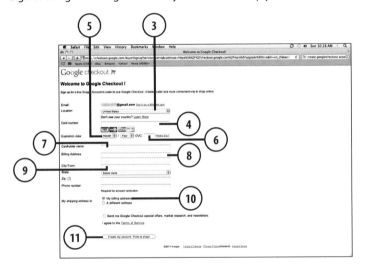

3. Choose your location.

4. Enter the credit card number with which you want to make purchases.

5. Select the credit card's expiration date.

6. Enter your card's CVV number (security code). This is a three- or four-digit number on the back of the card.

7. Enter your name.

8. Enter your billing address.

9. Enter your telephone number.

10. Select a shipping address.

11. Click Create My Account to complete the form. Now you are ready to make purchases on Android Market.

Searching for Android Applications

When you launch Android market, there are several ways to search apps from the Home page. The Home page search options change position on the page, depending on which orientation you hold your phone: vertical or horizontal.

1. Tap the Market widget to access Android Market. After you read the terms of service you can tap Accept.

2. Featured applications are listed on the Home page. Scroll up and down the page to review apps.

3. Tap an app to access a description page and read more about the product. You are given the opportunity to either purchase or download the app for free on the description page.

More About Product Descriptions

The description page for an app is chock full of useful information so that you can make an educated decision on whether you want to purchase the app. Sample screenshots of the app are featured on this page along with customer reviews and information about the developer.

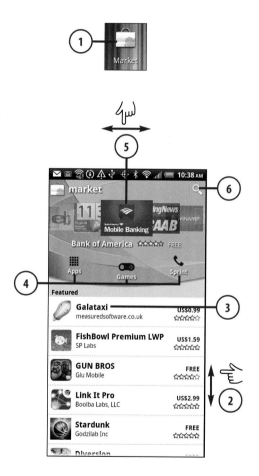

4. The Market home page also makes it possible to browse apps by categories: Apps, Games, and Sprint. Tap a category to browse the list of results.

5. Use your finger to flick through the list of popular apps featured horizontally at the top of the page. Tap an app to go to the product description page.

6. Tap the search icon to enter a search term.

7. Type a search term into the field. As you type, results appear in the list below.

8. Tap a search result to access the results page for that product. For example, if you selected a search for Angry Birds, you are taken to a results page that features all versions of that product.

9. Tap a result to access the product description page.

Finding Great Apps

There are thousands of apps you can download to your EVO 3D, so use your storage space wisely by finding great apps. Finding the best apps might be the biggest challenge of all, as you wade through your many options. The following are some tips on how to locate the highest performing apps.

1. Take a look at the featured apps on the Market homepage. When you access a category such as Apps or Games, review the Top Free and Top Paid categories. Keep in mind that large companies, usually with well-established names, tend to dominate the featured list. But less known developers are also producing outstanding apps, so look deeper.

2. Some apps have trial versions you can test drive before purchasing. Look for "Lite" or "Free" versions of applications to test before you buy.

3. When you locate an app you might want to purchase, scroll down to the bottom of the page and take a look at the Related section to find apps that are similar. Each app's rating is displayed next to the name of the app. You might find a higher-rated app you want to look into.

4. Check out customer reviews for products, but don't trust everything you read. Some reviews might not be in-depth or unbiased.

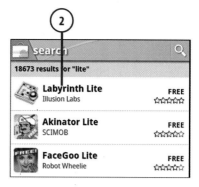

USING OTHER RESOURCES TO FIND APPS

There are other solid resources for you outside of the Android Market for finding great apps.

Perform a Google search. For example, if you are looking for an app suited for scanning barcodes, type "Barcode Scanner."

Search for sites that feature apps and post reviews. Be aware that some of these sites are sponsored by the developers and might not convey completely objective views.

Find an Android forum. There are many of these popping up every day. In a forum, you can post questions to other Android phone owners regarding apps. Beware that experienced Android users might not moderate all of these forums, and the advice you receive can be questionable.

Downloading Paid and Free Applications

Software developers from around the world have developed thousands of apps for you to take advantage of with your EVO 3D. There are many free apps to choose from in the Android Market, as well as a wide variety of more sophisticated apps that are available for a fee. The process for downloading free apps and paid apps is similar, but you need to designate a payment method to make purchases, as mentioned earlier in the chapter.

1. Tap the Market widget to access the Android Market.

2. Locate and then tap the app you want to purchase. The product description page opens.

More About Product Descriptions

The description page for an app is chock full of useful information so that you can make an educated decision on whether you want to purchase the app. Sample screen-shots of the app are featured on this page along with customer reviews and information about the developer. Be sure to tap More on the description page so that you review the complete description.

3. Tap the price of the app to see the permissions for this app. When the app is free, you tap the Free button.

4. Review the permissions and then tap OK to accept permissions. When the app is free, the down-loading process begins immedi-ately.

Accepting Permissions

If the application you have select-ed requires control of your phone or access to data, Market displays the information in this area. The list of permission changes from app to app. When you accept per-missions, you are essentially allowing the application you are purchasing to access your EVO 3D, including Internet access.

5. Tap in the Pay for This With field.

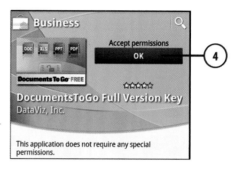

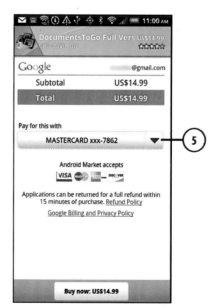

6. Tap the radial button next to the payment option you want to use.

7. Tap OK after you have chosen an option. If you choose the Bill My Sprint Account, you have to read a Carrier Billing consent form and then choose Accept.

8. If you chose Add a Credit Card, enter your credit card information and contact information into the provided fields.

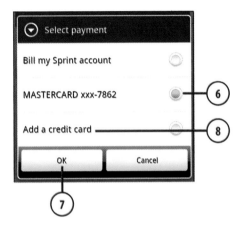

Removing a Credit Card

As of this publication, you cannot remove a credit card directly from your phone after you enter it as a payment option. You have to sign into your account at Google Checkout, https://checkout.google.com/, to edit your payment methods and remove the credit card.

9. Tap Buy Now to make the purchase and begin downloading the app. The app is downloaded and a shortcut is placed in your menu of apps.

Deleting Applications

There are a couple of ways you can delete an app you have purchased on Android Market from your EVO 3D if you no longer need it.

Deleting an Application Using Settings

You can go into the settings menu and uninstall applications on your phone. The following steps uninstall apps you have downloaded as well as those that were preinstalled on your EVO 3D.

Deleting Preinstalled Android Apps

Preinstalled Android applications are installed directly into the Android OS and not your EVO 3D's memory card like the apps you purchase on Android Market. There is no easy way to delete preinstalled apps from your phone. Be advised against attempting to uninstall any preinstalled Android apps.

1. Press the Menu button from a Home screen and then tap Settings.

2. Tap Applications.

3. Tap Manage Applications.

4. Select Downloaded to see all downloaded apps.

Filtering Results by Size

If you are looking to free up some memory space on your phone, you can press the Menu button on your EVO 3D and sort apps by storage size. This can help you locate apps that use the most space in case you can uninstall any of those.

5. Tap the application you want to delete.

6. Tap Uninstall.

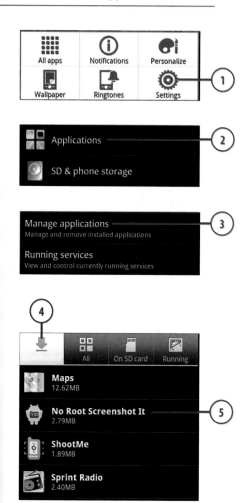

Deleting an Application Using Market

The second way to delete unwanted apps is by using the Uninstall option for the application in the Android Market app. With this method you can only delete apps you have downloaded within the Android Market app.

1. Tap the Android Market app on the Home screen.

2. From the Android Market's Home screen, press the Menu button on your EVO 3D and then tap My Apps.

3. Tap the application you want to uninstall.

4. Tap Uninstall. A warning message appears.

5. Tap OK in the warning message. The app is uninstalled.

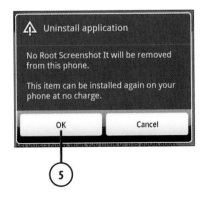

6. Select a reason why you are uninstalling the apps.

7. Tap OK.

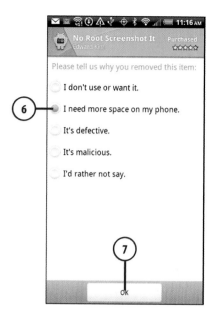

Keeping Applications Up to Date

Market periodically searches for updates for apps that you downloaded to your EVO 3D. If an update is found, a notification appears in the status bar in the top-left corner of your phone. You can drag the notifications panel down to reveal the updates. Tap an item in the list to go to Android Market so you can begin the update. You can also update downloaded apps from within Market.

1. Tap Market.

2. Press the Menu button and then tap My Apps.

3. Tap the app in the list you want to update or tap Update All at the top of the screen to perform all available updates.

4. If you tapped a single app on the list, you are taken to another screen. Tap Update.

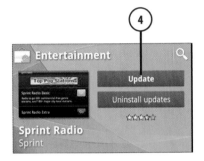

Customize your EVO 3D by
personalizing appearance
and settings

In this chapter, you find out how to customize your EVO 3D to fit your personal lifestyle. Topics include the following:

→ Changing your wallpaper
→ Using scenes
→ Changing your keyboard
→ Adding widgets to your home screen
→ Setting region and language
→ Using accessibility settings
→ Using search settings

Customizing Your EVO 3D

Your EVO 3D is a state-of-the-art entertainment center and productivity tool that can be customized to fit your own specific needs. There are a variety of settings at your disposal that enable you to personalize your EVO 3D and optimize its functions for your everyday life. In this chapter, you learn not only how to customize your phone's appearance, but also its functionality, including accessibility settings and search settings.

Changing Your Wallpaper

Perhaps the most basic customization you can perform with your EVO 3D is changing the default wallpaper. Your EVO 3D comes preloaded with several Google-designed wallpapers from which to choose, but you can also personalize your screen by choosing one of your own pictures.

1. Press the Menu button while on the Home screen and then tap Wallpaper.

2. Tap HTC wallpapers. The HTC Wallpaper Gallery appears.

3. You can tap Get More to purchase new wallpapers.

4. Flick through the gallery and then tap a wallpaper to preview it; alternatively, simply navigate to a wallpaper and then tap Preview at the bottom.

5. Tap Apply to switch your Home screen wallpaper. The wallpaper is applied, and you are taken back to the Home screen.

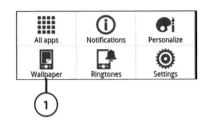

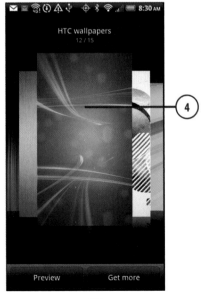

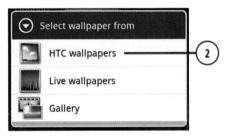

Live Wallpaper

Your EVO 3D is also preloaded with animated designs called Live Wallpaper that you can use to personalize the appearance of your Home screen. You can choose from cool designs such as a map that updates to your current location and is complete with traffic and weather info, a galaxy scene, a water scene, and grass blowing in the wind.

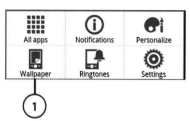

1. Press the Menu button while on the Home screen and then tap Wallpaper.

2. Tap Live Wallpapers. The Live Wallpapers Gallery opens.

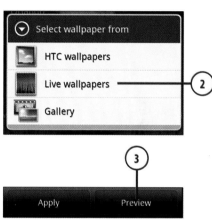

3. Flick through the wallpapers and then tap Preview to watch the animation.

4. Tap Settings to adjust the animation. Each animation comes with its own unique settings so that you can tweak the appearance.

5. Tap Apply to switch your Home screen wallpaper. The wallpaper is applied and you are taken back to the Home screen.

Wallpaper from Gallery Pictures

You can also apply photos that you have synced to your EVO 3D from your computer as wallpapers. Your EVO 3D is also a highly capable digital camera, so you can take your own images and use them as wallpaper for an added personal touch.

1. Press the Menu button while on the Home screen and then tap Wallpaper.

2. Tap Gallery. The albums of photos stored on your EVO 3D appear.

3. Tap the Gallery that has a photo you want to use.

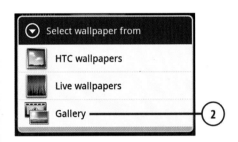

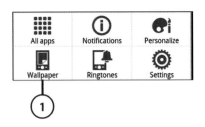

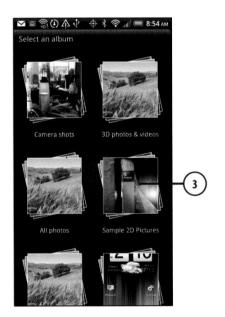

4. Tap the gallery photo you want to use. The photo opens full screen with a green cropping tool in the middle.

5. The green crop tool in the middle of the screen is confined to the dimensions of your EVO 3D screen. Drag the cropping tool and frame the part of the picture you want to use for the wallpaper. The cropping tool constrains the dimensions of the phone display as you drag.

6. Tap Save when you are finished. Your EVO 3D crops the photo and then applies it to the Home screen. You are taken back to the Home screen. This cropping process is nondestructive—the actual photo in the gallery is not cropped.

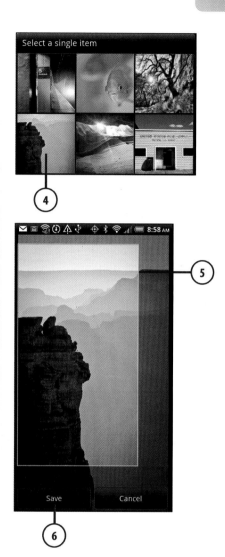

Using Scenes

Scenes differ from wallpaper in the way that they offer different widgets than your default Home screen. Look for a scene that comes with the widgets you use the most so you have faster access to the things you need.

Changing the Scene

To access more options for customizing your EVO 3D's Home and extended screens' appearance, you can tap the Personalize icon from any Home screen to access preloaded scenes, skins, and also Lock screen wallpaper designs.

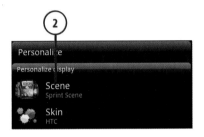

1. Tap the Personalize icon from the Home screen.

2. Tap Scene.

3. Flick through the designs and then tap Get More to purchase more Scenes.

4. After you find a scene you like, tap Apply. The scene is applied to the Home screen.

Creating Your Own Scene

You are not limited to the pre-designed scenes loaded on your phone; you can pick your own widgets, programs, and shortcuts, and rearrange existing items in a scene. After you create your own scene, you can save your creation.

1. Tap the Personalize icon from any Home screen.

2. Tap Scene.

3. Press the Menu button on Your EVO 3D.

4. Tap New.

5. Give the new scene a name.

6. Tap Done. You go to the Home screen with an empty wallpaper.

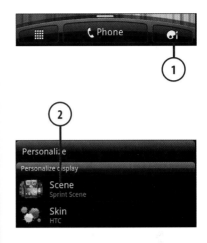

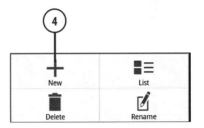

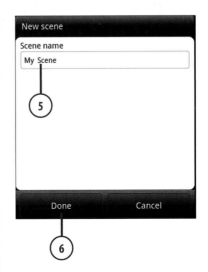

7. Change the wallpaper to the design you want and then add and arrange widgets to the wallpaper for all of your EVO 3D screens. The scene is automatically saved. Refer to the relevant sections about widgets and wallpaper in this chapter.

8. Your new creation is saved under Scenes. You can access it by following steps 1 and 2.

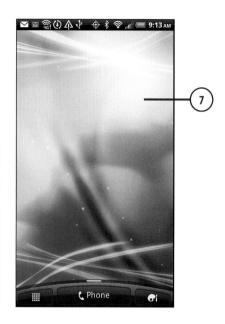

Renaming and Deleting Scenes

You can rename any theme by going to the Personalize menu, choosing Scene, and then holding your finger to a selected scene to access the Rename option. You can delete a theme by locating the scene, pressing the Menu button, and choosing Delete.

Using Skins

Skins enable you to apply an overall theme to not only the Home screen, but to extended screens as well. For example, if you choose the Blue Sky theme, the color scheme of the People app also changes. If you change the wallpaper, the skin you chose is still visible in other screens, such as in the People app.

1. Tap the Personalize icon from any Home screen.

2. Tap Skin.

3. Flick through the designs and tap Get More to purchase more skins.

4. After you find a skin you like, tap Apply. The scene is applied to the Home screen and to extended screens. Remember that you can change your wallpaper back, and the skin is still visible in other screens.

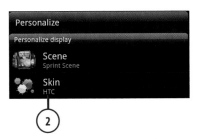

Changing the Lock Screen

The lock screen is the first screen you see when you wake your EVO 3D from sleep. You can also customize this screen with preloaded designs that utilize your photo album, stock market information, clock designs, and more.

1. Tap the Personalize icon from any Home screen.

2. Tap Lock Screen.

3. Flick through the designs and tap Settings to further customize the screen by choosing the shortcuts that appear on the new Lock screen. Each design has its own unique settings for you to tweak.

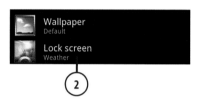

4. When you find a design you like and have chosen the shortcut and tweaked the settings, tap Done. For some designs, you are prompted to tap Select to choose a design option.

5. When you are finished, tap Apply. The design is applied to the Lock screen.

Changing Your Keyboard

If you find it difficult to type on your EVO 3D's default keyboard and you want a layout that better suits your typing style, there are three preloaded onscreen keyboard layouts you can choose from.

1. From a Home screen, press the Menu button and then choose Settings.

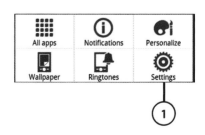

2. Scroll down and tap Language & Keyboard.

3. Tap Touch Input.

4. Tap Keyboard Types.

5. Tap Phone for a layout that resembles a traditional wireless phone keypad.

6. Tap Compact for a layout that features two letters on each key. The keys are larger than on the standard keyboard layout.

Before You Download a New Keyboard

If you desire a more stylish keyboard, there are Android developers who have developed replacement keyboards that you can download on Android Market. Make sure that you do your research before you download any replacement keyboard. When you install a nonstandard keyboard, your EVO 3D warns you that nonstandard keyboards have the potential for capturing each keyboard stroke you make. Make sure to research all prospective replacement keyboards before you download.

Swype Keyboard

The Swype keyboard offers an alternative approach to touch input keyboards that you might find easier for entering text on your EVO 3D. To type using the Swype keyboard, you trace your finger over the letters of the word you want to type. For example, if you want to type the word "and," put your finger on the *a* key on the keyboard and then trace the word by sliding your fingers across the remaining letters in the word "and" on the keyboard. Here is how you can switch the keyboard on your EVO 3D to the SWYPE keyboard.

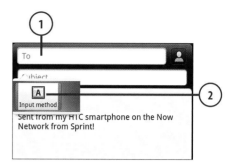

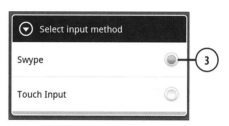

1. Within an application that lets you enter text, such as Mail and Messages, touch and hold your finger in the text box. A menu appears.

2. Tap Input Method.

3. Tap Swype. The input method switches to Swype.

4. To adjust the Swype settings, tap the Swype Key on the keyboard. A menu appears.

5. Tap Options to proceed to the Swype settings.

SWYPE BASICS

The Swype Settings menu on your EVO 3D offers a Swype tutorial if you need assistance in setting up and using it.

Type a word by swiping your finger across each character on the keyboard.

To type an uppercase letter, swipe over a letter, then swipe off the keyboard, and then swipe over the remaining characters in the word.

To type a double letter, circle the character on the keyboard.

If you type a word that is similar to a pre-existing word, the Swype keyboard displays a choice of possibilities. You then need to tap the word you want to use.

Trace Keyboard

Trace is an input method created by HTC that is very similar to Swype input. Like Swype, Trace enables you to swipe your fingers over letters to spell words without having to tap your fingers on the keyboard. Consider trying both the Swype and Trace inputs to evaluate the typing accuracy of each method.

1. From a Home screen, press the Menu button and then choose Settings.

2. Scroll down and tap Language & Keyboard.

3. Tap Touch Input.

4. Tap Trace Keyboard.

5. Tap to select the Trace Keyboard.

6. Tap to choose the pen color and stroke width when tracing letters on the keyboard.

Adding Widgets to a Home Screen

The Home screens are where you begin many of your activities on the EVO 3D. As you purchase new apps, you might be compelled to add them to a Home screen and then rearrange them according to the ones you use the most. Your EVO 3D comes with many widgets that you can add to your Home screens for quick access.

Adding a Widget

By default, when you download an application from the Android Market, a shortcut is placed in the Applications menu, which is accessible from any Home screen. You can easily add shortcuts from the Applications menu to a Home screen and then rearrange them. Your EVO 3D is equipped with useful widgets you can add to a Home screen by following a few simple steps.

1. Flick to the Home screen on which you want to add the widget.

2. Tap the Personalize icon.

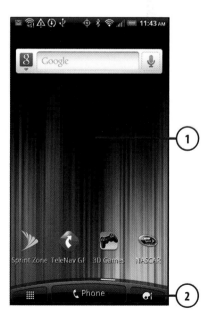

3. Tap Widget to access the list of available widgets on your EVO 3D.

4. Tap the widget you want to add. Some widgets offer various layouts and sizes you can choose from. If the widget you have chosen has more options, you are taken to a screen where you can select an option. If the widget does not have more options, it is immediately installed on a Home screen after you tap it.

5. The widget in this example has various layouts and sizes. Flick the screen to view the options.

6. Tap Details to read specifics about the widget's function.

7. Tap Select to add the widget to the Home screen.

Indicates more options are available for this widget

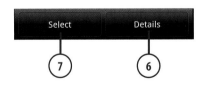

Moving a Widget

After adding widgets to your Home screen, you might want to rearrange them and move them to another screen. Here's how:

1. Touch and hold your finger on the widget you want to move.

2. Drag your finger around the screen. As you drag, a green box appears and indicates where you can move the widget. Most preexisting widgets on the screen move when you drag another widget on top of them, and then all widgets snap into place.

3. The green box turns red when you move it to areas onscreen that cannot accommodate the widget. You can drag the widget off screen to the left or right to place it on another screen.

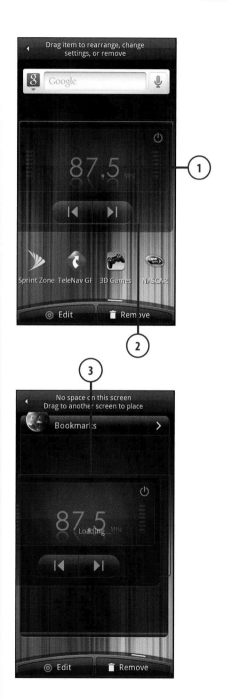

Removing a Widget

When you remove a shortcut or widget icon from a Home screen, it does not delete or uninstall the app from the EVO 3D; it simply removes it from that screen. If you want to add that widget again, it is still located in Widgets and the Applications menu. Here is how you remove a widget:

1. Touch and hold your finger on the widget you want to remove.

2. After the widget pulsates and your EVO 3D vibrates once, drag the widget to the word Remove at the bottom of the screen.

3. When the widget turns red, release it. The widget is removed from the Home screen.

Region and Language

Your EVO 3D enables you to change the language used if you move to another country. You can change the region and language in just a few steps.

1. Press the Menu button while on a Home screen and then tap Settings.

2. Scroll down and tap Language & Keyboard.

3. Tap Select Language.

4. Tap the language you want to switch to. Your EVO 3D switches to the language selected.

Switching to a New Language

All standard applications and menus immediately begin to use the new language as soon as you make the switch. Some third-party apps even use the new language, but many don't.

Accessibility Settings

There are no accessibility-related applications preinstalled on your EVO 3D, but you can download a screen reader for your phone from Android Market. If you follow the path where the accessibility options would be accessed on your phone, your EVO 3D has streamlined the process for installing the screen reader.

1. Press the Menu button while on a Home screen and then tap Settings.

2. Scroll down and tap Accessibility. An alert appears to inform you that there are currently no accessibility-related applications installed on your phone.

3. Tap OK to begin the process of downloading a screen reader to your EVO 3D.

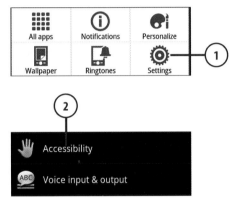

Search Settings

By default, when you perform a search from the Home screen on your EVO 3D, your phone searches content on your phone such as your contacts and Messages, as well as the Internet. You can configure the searchable items for your EVO 3D, including your music collection and call history.

1. Tap the Menu button while on a Home screen and then tap Settings.

2. Tap Search.

3. Tap Searchable Items. The Searchable Items list appears.

4. Select the searchable items you want to include in your search.

5. You can deselect previous searchable items to more narrowly focus your search.

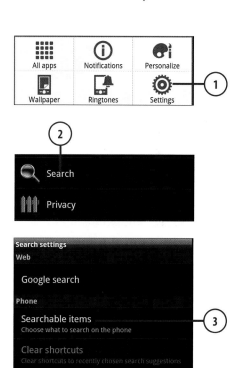

Maintain and troubleshoot EVO
3D software and hardware

This chapter covers ways you can properly maintain your HTC EVO 3D and troubleshoot basic software and hardware problems. Topics include the following:

- → Updating Android
- → Optimizing the battery
- → Dealing with problematic applications
- → Caring for your EVO 3D's exterior
- → Getting help with your EVO 3D

Maintaining and Troubleshooting Your EVO 3D

Although problems concerning the HTC EVO 3D Android software, hardware, and accessories are rare, on occasion you might experience incidents where your phone does not perform properly. There are a few fixes you can try if you experience the occasional glitch that can occur with any hardware device.

Updating Android

Every so often, Google releases software updates for your EVO 3D's Android operating system. To get the most from your phone, it is good practice to upgrade soon after an upgrade has been released. When an update is available, you receive a notification that indicates a system update is available. At that point, you have the options to Install Now, Install Later, or Discard.

1. A notification for an update appears in the status bar.

Manually Check for Updates

You can manually check for system updates by pressing the Menu button on your EVO and then tapping Settings, System Updates, and HTC Software Update. If there is an update available, follow the prompts to upgrade your software.

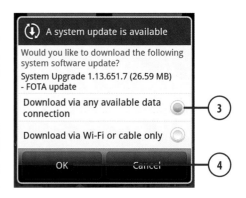

2. Pull down the Notification panel and then tap the system update. A message appears asking if you would like to download the update and prompts you to choose a connection type.

3. Select a connection type.

4. Tap OK.

5. A message might appear after you tap OK, informing you that additional data charges might apply if you do not have an unlimited data plan. If this message appears, tap Yes.

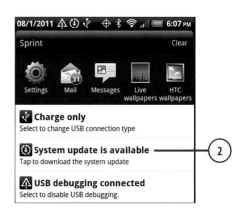

6. A message appears and asks you if would like to install the following system software update. Select Install Now.

7. Tap OK to begin the update.

Battery Optimizing

The lithium ion battery in your EVO 3D is capable of lasting battery life when you know how to take care of it. You can optimize the way you use your EVO 3D so that you can get the most life out of your battery and be able to use your phone for more hours throughout the day.

Take Care of the Battery

There are a few practices you can adopt to get the most from your EVO 3D battery. Knowing how to take care of your phone's battery can help it last longer.

1. Keep your phone's battery partially charged and avoid letting it fully discharge. Frequently allowing the battery to fully discharge can damage the battery. The key word in this tip is "frequently"; read step 2 for further clarification.

2. To avoid a false battery reading on your EVO 3D, perform a deep charge once every 30 charges to recalibrate the battery meter.

3. Avoid exposing your EVO 3D to extreme temperatures, which either hot or cold, have an effect on the performance of the battery and can cause damage.

4. Consider investing in multiple chargers for your EVO 3D. Instead of remembering to transport a single cable or wall jack, you can invest in one charger for home and another for work. This way, you always have the ability to charge your phone.

Extending Battery Life

Your EVO 3D is capable of acceptable battery life, but it can vary depending on how you use your phone. For example, more strenuous tasks such as recording and playing HD video will dramatically lower your battery life more than surfing the Web. You can monitor your battery power at the top of the screen in the Status area. The battery icon located in the right of the Status Bar enables you to keep an eye on how much battery power you have left. When the battery gets low, a warning appears informing you of the percent of battery power you have left and instructs you to connect the charger. When the battery is too low, your EVO 3D automatically shuts down.

In addition to the tips mentioned in the previous section, there are a few more things you can do to extend the life of your EVO 3D's battery.

Turn Off Radios

When the Wi-Fi and Bluetooth antennae are activated on your EVO 3D, your device is incessantly looking for available Wi-Fi networks to join and Bluetooth devices to pair with, which uses battery power. To see if Wi-Fi or Bluetooth radios are turned on, check in the Status Bar of your EVO 3D for both symbols. If you do not need a Wi-Fi connection and you are not using a Bluetooth device, turn these settings off to conserve battery power. You can easily turn off all radios in just a couple steps.

1. Flick the default Home screen from left to right.

2. Tap the Wi-Fi and Bluetooth options to turn them off. Both buttons should be grayed out after you deactivate them.

Bluetooth symbol   Wi-Fi symbol

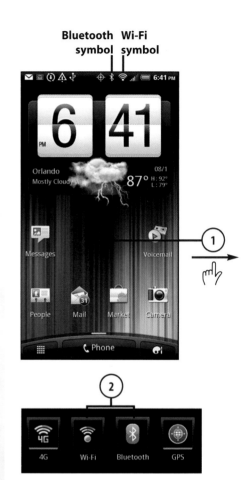

Dim Screen Brightness

The high-quality touchscreen of the EVO 3D can consume plenty of battery power. The higher the brightness level set on your EVO 3D, the more power the display uses. If you are viewing the screen in very bright conditions, you probably do not need a high brightness setting. Consider dimming the screen to extend the battery life.

1. Press the Menu button on your EVO 3D from any Home screen and then tap Settings.

2. Tap Display.

3. Tap Brightness to access the brightness controls.

4. Tap Automatic Brightness to deselect the settings. The brightness slider appears.

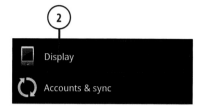

Automatic Brightness

When the Automatic brightness setting is selected, your phone uses sensors to determine your current light conditions and then adjusts the screen brightness automatically. In bright conditions, the screen is dimmed and vice versa.

5. Slide the slider to the left to lower the brightness level.

Utilize Sleep Mode

Your EVO 3D falls to sleep after a specified period of inactivity, but you don't have to wait for it to fall asleep—you can put it to sleep manually. When your phone is awake, it is consuming battery power. Press the Sleep button located on the top of your EVO 3D when you have finished using the device and conserve battery power.

Turn Off Vibration Settings

As you have probably noticed, by default, your EVO 3D vibrates using a tiny motor whenever you touch a button. Deactivating this feature will not help you conserve a significant amount of battery power, but it saves you something, which is better than nothing.

1. Press the Menu button on your EVO 3D from any Home screen and then tap Settings.

2. Choose Sound.

3. Tap Vibrate to deactivate the setting.

Monitor Power Usage

Your EVO 3D has a convenient screen
that lets you review which activities
have been consuming the most battery power. The types and number of
items that appear in the list depend
on the activities you have performed
on your phone between charges.
These activities could include using
the Maps app to get directions or
battery power used by Bluetooth.
Not every activity you perform
appears in the list.

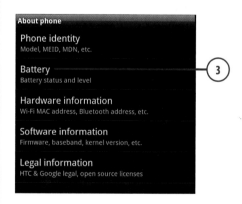

You can use the Battery Usage
screen to see which apps consume
the most power and then reduce the
use of those apps. Your battery
power savings will be small, but if
you're running low on power, with
no way to recharge, every little bit
counts. Follow these directions to
access the Battery Usage screen.

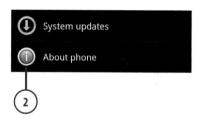

1. Press the Menu button from any
   Home screen and then tap
   Settings.

2. Scroll down and then tap About
   Phone.

3. Tap Battery.

4. Select Battery Use.

Task Killers

The more apps you have running, the more battery power your EVO 3D consumes. When you close an app on your phone, it keeps running in the background. You can manually stop an app from running from within one of these apps. To find a task-killing app, just go to the Android Market application and perform a search for "task killer" or "task manager." Many of these apps are free. You can also use your EVO 3Ds built-in Manage Applications function to kill a task. Read the following task to learn how to use this function.

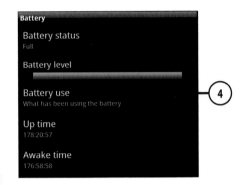

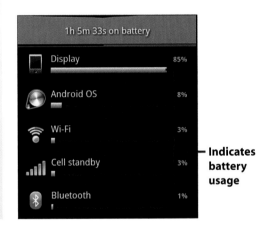

Indicates battery usage

Force Stop a Problematic App

Sometimes an app can get an attitude and become unruly. For example, an app that provides a warning screen saying that it is currently busy and is unresponsive or gives some other issue warning conveying there is a problem. If an app is giving you problems, you can manually stop the app. After you stop it, try launching it again to see if it works correctly. Follow these steps to force stop an unruly app.

1. Press the Menu button from a Home screen and then tap Settings.

2. Scroll down and then tap Applications.

3. Touch Manage Applications.

4. Tap Running to filter the results to apps that are currently running.

5. Tap the app in the list that you want to stop.

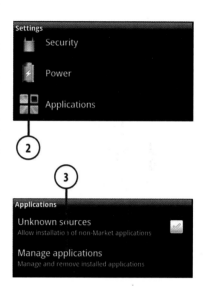

6. Tap Stop. The app stops running.

Caring for the EVO 3D's Exterior

Regular maintenance of your EVO 3D not only helps you extend the life of your phone, but also helps ensure peak performance of your device. Making sure your EVO 3D software is up to date and understanding basic troubleshooting concepts is important, but properly cleaning and protecting your phone's body can be equally important. The EVO 3D was designed to be sturdy, but just like any other electronic device, it can collect dust, and a simple drop on the sidewalk can prove disastrous. The first step in maintaining your EVO 3D is prevention. You can start by purchasing a protective case.

A sturdy case designed for the EVO 3D is important for the overall protection of your device. A number of companies have created a variety of cases for the EVO 3D, so perform a Google search or go to Amazon to see what's out there. The more padded the case, the better it can absorb a shock if you happen to drop your phone. A case can also help protect your phone from dust and keep it dry if you happen to get caught out in the rain. Make sure you keep the inside of your case clean. Dust and sand can find its way into even the most well-constructed cases. Instead of using your sleeve to wipe off your EVO 3D's display, invest in a microfiber cloth that you can find in any office supply or computer store.

Your first instinct might be to wet a cloth to clean your EVO 3D touchscreen. Don't use liquids—especially alcohol and ammonia—to clean the phone's touchscreen. These harsh chemicals can cause irreparable damage to the touchscreen, rendering it difficult to see. Consider purchasing a screen protector at your local Best Buy or cellular store to keep the touchscreen dust and scratch free. Some screen protectors also come with a microfiber cleaning cloth.

Getting Help with Your EVO 3D

Sprint support, (800) 639-6111 or http://support.sprint.com, and the Official Google website, http://android.com/, are great resources for getting help with technical issues regarding your EVO 3D. Also check out some popular Android blogs:

- Android Central at http://www.androidcentral.com/

- Android Guys at http://www.androidguys.com/

- Androinica at http://androinica.com/

Index

LIKE THIS BOOK? CHECK OUT OTHER TITLES IN THIS SERIES

ISBN 13: 9780789742551   ISBN 13: 9780789742858   ISBN 13: 9780789744715   ISBN 13: 9780789747143

Full-Color, Step-by-Step Guides

The "My..." series is a visually rich, task-based series to help you get up and running with your new device and technology and tap into some of the hidden, or less obvious features. The organized, task-based format allows you to quickly and easily find exactly the task you want to accomplish, and then shows you how to achieve it with minimal text and plenty of visual cues.

Visit quepublishing.com/mybooks to learn more about the My... book series from Que.

quepublishing.com

 Safari
Books Online

FREE
Online Edition

Your purchase of *My HTC EVO™ 3D* includes access to a free online edition for 45 days through the **Safari Books Online** subscription service. Nearly every Que book is available online through **Safari Books Online**, along with thousands of books and videos from publishers such as Addison-Wesley Professional, Cisco Press, Exam Cram, IBM Press, O'Reilly Media, Prentice Hall, and Sams.

Safari Books Online is a digital library providing searchable, on-demand access to thousands of technology, digital media, and professional development books and videos from leading publishers. With one monthly or yearly subscription price, you get unlimited access to learning tools and information on topics including mobile app and software development, tips and tricks on using your favorite gadgets, networking, project management, graphic design, and much more.

Activate your FREE Online Edition at
informit.com/safarifree

STEP 1: Enter the coupon code: HNNVFWH.

STEP 2: New Safari users, complete the brief registration form.
Safari subscribers, just log in.

If you have difficulty registering on Safari or accessing the online edition,
please e-mail customer-service@safaribooksonline.com